INSTANT DIVINE ASSISTANCE

Your Complete Guide
to Fast and Easy
Spiritual Awakening,
Healing, and More

Benjamin Bernstein

PRAISE FOR THE INVOCATIONS YOU'LL LEARN IN THIS BOOK

"After I did [Benjamin's] invocation, **it felt like God rushing in!**"

— Rose Vanyo

"I've been using Benjamin's invocations for over two years, and have had amazing results. I've had some **very deep healing experiences with repressed material.… Out of all the healings I've done on myself over the years, Benjamin's Healing Invocation is the topper**."

— Pam Chapman

"I have been using Benjamin's invocations on a daily basis for over ten years. **They've really helped me overcome my anxiety and lack of self-confidence.** They also **help me sleep at night** when I get insomnia.… One has really **helped me make the right decisions** over the last ten years, and has made my life easier and more enjoyable."

— Mark Okrasa

"So many wonderful things have happened since my work with Benjamin's invocations! **I have written two books and am** working on a third. I've purchased a home. And I've developed many friendships and co-creative partnerships.

"Invoking saturation of the healing love and light is so powerful. It burns away the obstacles that prevent me from moving forward, feeling connected, and creating a rewarding life."

— Hannah Desmond

"I smoked for many years, and my lungs were so damaged that I couldn't take a deep breath. It hurt just to breathe!

"But after doing the invocations for a few months, I was walking on the beach one morning and suddenly realized that I was taking deep, full breaths — with no pain."

— Amanda Elwell

"**I used the Healing Invocation**, and felt this pain open up in my chest. **I felt immense relief** and started crying. **I felt the pain just melt out of me.**

"It was so helpful to process the pain from that breakup. **It was so empowering to know that my higher self and I could heal it. I didn't need anything external. I didn't need to pay for anything. I didn't need to talk to any other human. It all happened within me.**

"At first, I was so surprised that these invocations worked. It makes me wonder what other amazing possibilities that I can't even imagine might open to me as I keep using them!"

— Emily

"**Benjamin's Healing Invocation ... completely dissipated [a childhood wound's] traumatic energy**.... The Healing Invocation has helped me **about 80 percent more effectively** than any other healing tool or technique I've tried!"

— Brian Scotti

"[Benjamin's invocations] allowed me to finally feel a complete 'rest' of my soul. **At long last, I didn't feel all the hurt, shame, blame, frustration, and anger that had been so hard to deal with.... I now feel connected to my spirit team at all times**.... I can always use Benjamin's invocations to help ground me and find my inner calmness."

— Beverly Rickard

"**The invocations helped release patterns and stuck emotions that were ready to transmute — and they did it fast!** ... [They] have **helped my awakening and channeling abilities expand immensely**."

— Chloé

"**Benjamin's invocations ... allowed me to access a different dimension within myself** that I never even knew existed ... quieting my mind, healing my body, and allowing my spirit to pervade ... **I now know my potential is boundless!**"

— Starla K.

Copyright © 2022 Benjamin Bernstein

All rights reserved.

ISBN 979-8-9867032-0-6 (Paperback Edition)

Edited by Reedsy Editor Catherine J. Rourke.

Book cover by Sanjeev Gupta, grafixland.com.

Printed and bound in the United States of America.

First printing October 2022.

Any advice or recommendations are made without guarantee on the part of the author or publisher. The author and publisher disclaim any liability in connection with the use of the information in this book. The information presented is the author's opinion and does not constitute medical or health advice and is not intended to diagnose, treat, cure, or prevent any condition or disease. The ideas and suggestions in this book are not meant to be a substitute for seeking professional guidance. Please consult your physician.

benjamin@astroshaman.com

Visit InstantDivineAssistance.com.

CONTENTS

Title Page
Praise for the Invocations You'll Learn in This Book
Copyright
Preface   1
Part One: Foundational Information   3
Chapter One: Big Picture Overview   4
Chapter Two: The Embodied Awakening Invocation   14
Chapter Three: The Healing Invocation   29
Chapter Four: IDA Invocation Daily Maintenance   48
Chapter Five: Four Ways to Use the Healing Invocation   53
Chapter Six: The Hollow Reed Invocation: How to Be a Conduit for Highest Good Energy   68
Chapter Seven: Invocation Construction Kit   80
Chapter Eight: Consistency and Amnesia   90
Part Two: Diving Deeper   103
Chapter Nine: The Embodied Awakening Invocation Cycle   104
Chapter Ten: Invocations for Specific Challenges   114
Chapter Eleven: Support to Stay on Track   145
Chapter Twelve: Final Thoughts   155
Appendix A: The Main Invocations in This Book   161

Appendix B: Key Takeaways	163
Appendix C: Resources and Websites Mentioned in this Book	188
Gratitude	191
About the Author	193

PREFACE

What you learn in this book might seem too good to be true.

That certainly would have been my response — before I experienced the Instant Divine Assistance (IDA) Invocations for myself.

It might be hard to believe that you can experience spiritual awakening within seconds — just by requesting it from your higher self.

It might seem incredible that you could quickly and permanently heal a serious challenge — even one that's caused you years of physical, emotional, or mental suffering — by delegating the work to your inner healer.

It might seem crazy to think that your higher self stands ready to fill you up with any kind of energy you want — whenever you want it.

And it might seem far-fetched that you could have divine energy flow through you to powerfully heal and bless others — simply by calling it in and being a "hollow reed."

I welcome your skepticism. But a healthy skeptic isn't just cautious. They're also curious and open-minded.

I won't ask you to take anything on faith. If the IDA Invocations work for you, you'll definitely know!

All the information you need to master the Instant Divine Assistance Invocations is in this book. I've held nothing back.

At the same time, I've deliberately made this book lean and focused. I know your time is valuable. You won't have to slog through a bunch of fluff or padding.

Are you ready to make "too good to be true" your "new normal"? Read on!

PART ONE: FOUNDATIONAL INFORMATION

CHAPTER ONE: BIG PICTURE OVERVIEW

I've been working with the Instant Divine Assistance Invocations for over eleven years. In that time, I've used them successfully with thousands of people.

Here are short quotes from four of them. These will give you a sense of how these invocations might also help you!

> I discovered Benjamin's invocations in 2012. They cleared a major energetic blockage and opened up a huge awakening to the next level of my divine consciousness.
>
> I still use his invocations daily to connect to Source, and have my day guided for the best intentions for all. I quote him often: "My ego is in the passenger seat, and Source is driving!"
>
> — Donna Clifford

During my first experience with Benjamin's Healing Invocation, I felt all the animosity I had formerly felt completely dissipate. I felt light and sweet. I was so elated that I stayed awake late into the night, with no need for sleep.

The next day, when I thought of the trauma that left, I had no inkling of hurt or animosity. Wow!

— Malu Buckmaster

I was feeling isolated because of the pandemic. Many of my friends relocated, and a few passed from the physical realm. The usual places I would go and the things I did with others were not happening.

But when I used Benjamin's invocations, I felt myself surrounded and supported by my divine allies. This brings a great feeling of comfort and peace. I no longer feel that I walk totally alone. I invite the allies in and thank them.

I make this an ongoing practice. It always helps me feel better right away and keeps a sense of connectedness within me.

— JW

Benjamin's invocations have been extremely beneficial in allowing me to stay grounded and clear when traumas or difficulties arise. I feel more fluid moving through them. The invocations are simple and easy to use, and they've been such a blessing and support in my life!

— Vanessa Johnson

The Life-Transforming Techniques You'll Learn

Here's what you'll learn in this book:

The **Embodied Awakening Invocation**. First, you'll learn its four life-transforming benefits — each one a game-changer. Then you'll experience how fast and easy it is to merge your higher self and your human self into a single euphoric consciousness.

You'll also get a link to a **free recording** where I'll lead you through the Embodied Awakening Invocation on video or audio. (This book also has links to other valuable online resources that will help speed up your personal evolution. And most of them are free!)

Next, you'll learn about the **Healing Invocation**. This lets you call in healing from your higher self… and lets it do the healing for you! Once again, a link will lead to free video and audio of me guiding you through this powerful process. This will allow you to experience divinely delegated healing for yourself.

Then you'll learn about **daily maintenance**. You'll discover how to easily weave these two foundational invocations into your life. *This simple everyday practice will take almost no time or effort.*

At this point, you'll know your IDA Invocation basics. You'll be ready to dive deeper!

The Healing Invocation has two additional variations. You'll learn how these can help you.

The IDA Invocations can also help others. The next section will teach you **how to effortlessly flow divine light to others for their highest good**.

After that, it's time to get creative and roll your own. With the **Invocation Construction Kit**, you can create your own invocations as needed. Call in whatever energy you want or need!

Then we'll get into **consistency and amnesia**. You'll learn how to avoid losing awareness of your spiritual self. This lets you avoid the suffering that always comes with this forgetfulness.

What if amnesia already has you in its grip? My **reawakening strategies** can help you regain embodied awakening.

Next, you'll gain deeper mastery of the IDA Invocations.

The Embodied Awakening Invocation is a super-efficient shortcut. It's like a speedboat racing you to your destination.

But what if you want to slow down and enjoy a luxury cruise? You can do the **four-step Embodied Awakening Invocation Cycle**. It lets you:

> 1. Call your higher self to saturate you with all the light and divine consciousness that serves your highest good;
>
> 2. Become one with your higher self *beyond* your physical body and bask in that ecstasy;
>
> 3. Invite your higher self to merge with you *in* your physical body; and,
>
> 4. Invoke the deepest ongoing integration of your higher self and physical body that serves highest good. The benefits of this are priceless!

Next, you'll learn **invocations for specific challenges**. These include letting go, life direction, relationships, sleep, alertness, and work. You'll also learn invocations that can help with specific psychological challenges, 12-Step programs, and the seven chakras.

You'll learn about **free support that can help you stay on track with your invocation practice**. These include reminder emails, invocation challenges, an accountability partner, and a free bonus chapter.

Finally, in the appendices, you'll get **the main invocations from this book collected in one place**, and **Key Takeaways for Chapters Two through Eleven**. These could give you the essential information you need when you return to this book, and could eliminate the need to reread an entire chapter.

In short, you're about to learn a tremendous amount of life-transforming information!

In my experience, the IDA Invocations work over 99 percent of the time, with all kinds of people. Even if you don't achieve full embodied awakening or get a complete and final healing, the rewards can still improve your life profoundly!

How the IDA Invocations Found Me

I didn't really discover the Instant Divine Assistance Invocations. It's more like they found me! They just dropped into my brain in a magical moment of divine inspiration.

I had no idea they were coming. But I had set the stage without knowing it.

I was attending a two-night ayahuasca ceremony in upstate New York. It was a New Year's event, on a frigid weekend that transitioned from 2010 to 2011.

Ayahuasca is a psychoactive indigenous medicine from South America. I've done over 250 plant spirit ceremonies, mostly with this "vine of the soul," for over sixteen years.

Ayahuasca is an extraordinary ally for me. She supercharges my healing, awakening, and ability to serve others. I feel incredibly fortunate that I can work with this sacred and life-transforming medicine, and always do so with profound reverence.

Don't worry. You won't have to drink ayahuasca or take psychedelics to do these invocations. But I want to give credit where it's due!

I took notes after that weekend's first ceremony, which was on the final day of 2010. Here are the two most striking excerpts:

> I felt so close to reaching enlightenment! I got a brief experience, but it was fleeting. Toward ceremony's end, I declared several times that I was ready for awakening if it would serve my highest need.

> Late in the ceremony, I saw a new star shine forth in the vision's night sky. It looked like the Star of Bethlehem. My sense was that this represented my awakening, and the light that I would radiate to the world to assist others.

Clearly, spiritual awakening was on my mind. But this was nothing new. I'd been chasing enlightenment for thirty-five years!

Inspiration Strikes

But inspiration actually struck on New Year's Day of 2011.

During that second ceremony, Mother Ayahuasca downloaded the Instant Divine Assistance Invocations into my brain. She showed me how to call in healing and embodied awakening. She also showed me how to invoke any kind of energy I want!

Dazzled by this new information, I immediately invoked my own embodied awakening. It worked like a charm, bringing my higher self down to merge seamlessly with my human self. I experienced a profound spiritual awakening: a blissful state of higher consciousness and divine union.

The invocation had worked for me. But would it be effective for anyone else?

I decided to find out. After the ceremony closed, I told the woman sitting to my left what had happened. She agreed to try the Embodied Awakening Invocation. I led her through it, and she was delighted to report that it worked for her within seconds.

Three other ceremony participants watched me work with her. They also wanted to try the invocation, so I led them through it as a group. They all said they moved quickly and easily into embodied awakening.

This was an awesome start. Then again, we were all under the influence of ayahuasca!

Fortunately, the invocations have demonstrated their effectiveness ever since. This has proved true even when people are stone-cold sober, or have never meditated a day in their lives.

And the Instant Divine Assistance Invocations have certainly been useful to me! Each time ayahuasca has awakened me more deeply, I've used the invocations to stabilize each new level as my "new normal."

So, that's how the IDA Invocations were born.

And that's one of the longest stories I'll be telling about myself.

Self-help books often open with a story of the author heroically mastering a life-threatening crisis. If I'd had such an experience, I'd be telling you about it right now.

But I haven't. My spiritual path has been more about relentless persistence than "dark night of the soul" drama.

So, this isn't one of those books where you come to learn something useful, but then have to slog through page after page of the author prattling on about themselves.

That's one reason most of the true-life stories in this book are from other people. Their experiences show how their lives improve, often dramatically, when they use the IDA Invocations. I hope their stories get you excited about how these invocations can also help you!

IDA Musings

When choosing a name for this invocation system, I wanted it to be simple, clear, and easy to understand. "Instant Divine Assistance" fit the bill.

"Instant Divine Assistance" also made an acronym I liked: "IDA." But it wasn't until weeks later, when I finally researched the name "Ida," that I realized just how well-suited it is!

Ida is a German name meaning "industrious one" or "hardworking." This perfectly describes how ready and willing your higher self is to do all the heavy lifting for you when you invoke it.

Mount Ida, on Crete, is the mythological birthplace of Zeus. This associates "Ida" with the immense power of the king of the Greek gods, and hints at how much power these invocations make available to you! Ida is also the name of a nymph who nursed baby Zeus — just as your higher self will lovingly nurture you when you ask.

In Hindu mythology, Ida is a goddess of speech — the preferred method of invocation. And Ida is thought to derive from an Old English expression for "prosperous, happy." These invocations can definitely help you achieve that!

IDA also stands for "Initial Distress Alert." Ships in trouble send these to get help from the Coast Guard or Air Force. You, even more easily, can receive Instant Divine Assistance from your higher self as soon as you need it.

Finally, as a punster, I love that the name has wordplay potential. You can use the Instant Divine Assistance Invocations — then, as your higher self does everything for you, sit "IDA-ly" by!

IDA like to mention one more thing about this name. The stories from others in this book never mention "IDA Invocations." Instead, they usually say "Benjamin's invocations." This is because, at the time I received these stories, I hadn't come up with the "IDA Invocations" name yet.

Find a Mistake? Email Me!

Perfection is impossible, but I try anyway! I've corrected all the mistakes I could find in this book, but I've almost certainly missed some. If you discover any errors, please email me at benjamin@astroshaman.com. I can easily correct them so future readers will have a better experience.

You now have an overview of what you'll learn in this book. And you know how the IDA invocations were born.

Let's move on to Chapter Two, where you can experience their extraordinary benefits for yourself!

CHAPTER TWO: THE EMBODIED AWAKENING INVOCATION

The Embodied Awakening Invocation is the best DIY technique I know to call in spiritual awakening. Even after more than eleven years, it remains a cornerstone of my daily spiritual practice.

What does "embodied awakening" mean? At the most basic level, it simply means *you're consciously aware of your higher self merged with your physical body*. As Donna said, it's as if your physical body is a car, and your human self is delighted to let your higher self drive.

You'll understand "embodied awakening" better as you keep reading. In fact, here are….

Four Major Benefits

You'll enjoy four major benefits when you're in embodied

awakening. If you make it your "new normal" (see Chapter Four), you'll be constantly rewarded with these life-enhancing benefits:

1. You'll enjoy more harmony, flow, ease, and grace. Instead of being overwhelmed by challenging thoughts and emotions, you'll stay calm more consistently.

2. Whatever you're responsible for, you'll do *more* responsibly — and more joyfully!

3. Instead of always having to figure things out, you'll increasingly know what to do through intuition.

4. You'll feel more euphoria!

There are lots of other benefits. But many are impossible to put into words since they're beyond the field of mind.

Then again, Starla does a good job describing her experience:

> I had been on a path of healing and introspection for about six months before I found Benjamin's "Awakening Plus" online community. I began as an attendee of his weekly "New Earth Support Team" Zoom calls.
>
> Benjamin's invocations and passive body-awareness techniques were a catalyst that accelerated my healing to the next level. His invocations allowed me to access a different dimension within myself that I never even knew existed. It's a space that has evoked a transformative shift in my overall well-being by quieting my mind, healing my body, and allowing my spirit to pervade.
>
> I'm eternally grateful to Benjamin for awakening my awareness. I now know my potential is boundless!

— Starla K.

A level of consciousness can't comprehend a level beyond itself. So, there's no way to *fully* understand what Starla is talking about — or what I'm about to describe — until you experience it. Just stay with me the best you can.

Let Your Higher Self Drive

Let's expand on my automotive metaphor. If you aren't in embodied awakening, it's as if your body is a car and your ego is driving. Once you do the Embodied Awakening Invocation, your ego moves to the passenger seat. And your higher self gets in and drives.

Your ego is still in charge. Your higher self can only stay with its permission. If your ego doesn't like its driving, it can instantly take the wheel again. Your higher self will step right out with no fuss, returning full control to your ego.

Let me emphasize this, so your ego really gets it. **Your ego is in no danger. There's no risk. You can instantly go back to the way it was. Your ego is perfectly safe!**

Housebreaking Your Ego

Some spiritual paths say you must kill your ego to attain awakening. Is it any surprise your ego would rebel against this idea? It believes it's fighting for its life!

I prefer to think of my ego getting *housebroken*. Unawakened egos can be like untrained puppies. You never know when they'll tear through the house, pee on the floor, or hump somebody's leg.

At first, my ego resisted awakening. It was terrified of losing control.

But as my ego began letting my higher self drive, it started to *prefer* the passenger seat. There's a reason some people hire chauffeurs. It's so much easier when someone else drives!

My ego didn't just appreciate the huge amount of effort it was saving. It also quickly realized how *smart* my higher self is.

You could be the smartest human on earth. But your ego would still be like the slowest kid in class compared to the vastly superior intelligence of your higher self. Your ego thinks, but your higher self *knows*!

With this understanding, is your ego willing to give the Embodied Awakening Invocation a test drive?

Let My Voice Guide You

At first, most people find this invocation easier when my voice guides them. Go to InstantDivineAssistance.com for a free recording of me guiding you through this process step by step.

This recording is helpful because you get the instructions without having to read them. But there's also an *energetic* benefit. I was in embodied awakening when I made the recording, so the recording transmits that frequency.

This makes it easier for you to attain this euphoric state, especially when you're just getting started. It's almost as good as me guiding you in person!

This recording, available on audio and video, is like the training wheels on a bicycle. Once you get the hang of the invocation, you won't need the recording anymore.

Your body position doesn't matter when you do the Embodied Awakening Invocation. You can be standing, sitting, reclining, laying down — whatever. The only requirement is that you can focus your attention. And it's ideal to be as relaxed as possible.

It's best to do this with your eyes closed. This is because your brain devotes most of its energy to visual processing. Having your eyes open would distract most of your attention. If you're reading these instructions, close your eyes whenever you can.

Step-by-step instructions follow, supplemented with helpful information. If you just want bare-bones instructions, they're at the end of this chapter.

Let everything else go. Become aware of your whole body at once.

If you have awareness of subtle energy in your body, just feel it. Don't change or fix anything. Just notice where you're starting from. Later, you can recall this baseline feeling to notice how your energy has changed.

You're about to speak to your higher self. This divine part of you created your human part. Your higher self is always watching over it. Your higher self is always happy to help and will *always* come when you call!

If you don't like the term "higher self," you can use "divine self," "soul," or whatever feels good to you.

What if you aren't comfortable with the idea that a part of you is divine? Fortunately, this invocation will also work if you call on an external divine being such as Jesus Christ or your guardian angel. As long as you let divine consciousness merge with your human consciousness, you're good. It's like the old joke: "I don't care what you call me, just don't call me late for dinner!"

How to Do the Embodied Awakening Invocation

You're almost ready to learn this eight-word invocation. But first, let me explain a two-word phrase in it. *"Highest good" is shorthand for "my highest good, and the highest good of all those affected by this."*

It would be more grammatically correct to say "*the* highest good." But I prefer short invocations. As long as the meaning is clear, I delete every nonessential word.

It's finally time to do the Embodied Awakening Invocation. Say it out loud if you can, or think it silently if you must:

"Maximum embodied awakening that serves highest good, please."

Let the words go. Now you'll choose what to focus on. You have two choices.

First, notice if you feel subtle energy moving in your body. This energy has many names, including *chi*, *prana* and *life force*. It might tingle or feel like a flow inside you. If you feel this subtle energy, even slightly, make it your focus.

If you don't feel subtle energy, focus on breath sensation. As the breath comes and goes on its own, notice where you feel it most easily. The nostrils? Head? Throat? Chest? Stomach? Gently focus your attention there.

Let your breath come easily and naturally. It doesn't matter if it's fast or slow, shallow or deep. *Don't use any breath control.* Just notice the sensation, while staying 100 percent passive.

While the invocation is filling you with energy…

>Don't make anything happen with effort or willpower.

>Don't *stop* anything from happening.

>Don't *deliberately* visualize or imagine anything.

When Helping Isn't Helpful

After you say the Embodied Awakening Invocation, rest in passive awareness of subtle energy or breath. That's the *only* thing you should be doing.

If you use effort or willpower, your higher self will notice. Then, because of the Law of Free Will, it will stop helping you or help much less. Fortunately, the instant you become passive, your higher self will be right there helping you again.

Some spiritual practices require the ego to direct energy. The IDA Invocations don't. You'll get vastly better results if you *avoid* using effort or willpower. Just relax and let your higher self do everything for you.

Imagine you've hired the world's finest chef to cook a gourmet meal for you. Would you hover over them in the kitchen, specifying what ingredients to use and how to prepare them? I hope not!

In the same way, your higher self is the energy work expert. Once you've said your invocation, your best strategy is to chill out and wait at the table. Let your higher self bring that exquisitely prepared meal to you on a golden platter!

In the same spirit of passivity, don't deliberately visualize or imagine these invocations working. That's just more effort that will gum up the works.

If you *spontaneously* see colors or visions, that's fine. Just treat them as distractions. Speaking of which....

Distractions

If your attention is anywhere except your chosen focus, treat it as a distraction. I recommend this response:

> Don't fight the distraction.
>
> Don't try to change it.
>
> Let it be exactly as it is, with no resistance.

For our purposes, *the distraction isn't you*. It's an uninvited guest, so give it no further attention. If you do, you'll only feed it energy and make it stronger.

Having noticed the distraction, return your focus to subtle energy or breath. Keep doing this very gently and persistently, as often as necessary.

If the distraction continues, that's perfectly fine. Let it do its thing in the background, while you continuously return to your chosen focus.

It doesn't matter how many times you get distracted or how long the distractions last. Just follow this simple guideline: *each time you get distracted, return to passive awareness, gently and persistently*. Your best effort is always good enough!

Any Thought at All

Distractions include any thought at all — *even if the thought seems helpful.*

From a spiritual perspective, all mental activity creates static. This runs interference with divine energy when doing this invocation.

Passive awareness of energy or breath is a *non-mental* focus. It lets divine energy enter freely.

If you're fully immersed in feeling energy or breath, there won't be any mental chatter.

Most people have only one point of awareness available. If it's 100-percent focused on passive awareness, there won't be any space for thought. Every time you find yourself thinking, refocus on passive awareness instead.

What if you can hold multiple points of awareness at the same time? This is obviously more advanced. If you can do this *spontaneously* and *effortlessly*, more power to you! But if doing this keeps you from getting the maximum benefit from the invocation, hold one point of awareness instead.

Finally, *invocations aren't mantras. Repeating them won't make them more effective.* There's no need to say them more than once during each invocation process. Your higher self heard you the first time!

The Minimum Effort Game

To achieve embodied awakening, persistently returning to your chosen focus may be all you need. If so, that's wonderful. I always prefer the simplest path to success!

But there's one more nuance you can bring to this process: the Minimum Effort Game. This might make this invocation even more effective.

The idea here is to use the *least possible effort* that keeps your focus on subtle energy or breath.

Try it now. For just a moment, drop to zero effort. Simply exist. Be completely passive. Whatever happens is fine.

After a moment, notice if you're *effortlessly* aware of your chosen focus. If it's subtle energy, can you feel it moving in your body? If it's breath, can you feel inhalation and exhalation happening on its own? *If this is happening with zero effort, stay at zero.*

But what if dropping to zero effort makes you *lose* this awareness?

Then start adding teeny-tiny bits of effort. These micro-efforts are like the gentlest touch of a feather. Keep adding these until you *just barely* regain awareness of your chosen focus.

Feel free to play with your effort level — adding or subtracting micro-bits of effort — until you find *the absolute least effort that holds your chosen focus.* This "sweet spot" leaves maximum space for the divine to help you.

How to Know When You're in Embodied Awakening

Sometimes embodied awakening locks in right away. Other times it might take a while. The more you do it, the easier it gets.

How will you know you're in embodied awakening? Four things will be true at the same time:

1. No mental chatter.

2. No challenging emotion.

3. You'll feel peaceful.

4. All this will be completely effortless.

Once all four things are true, your light body has merged with your physical body.

You may also notice a *subtle tingling*. This is how your higher self feels in your physical body. But even if you aren't tingling, you can still be in embodied awakening.

Another nuance is that *your consciousness isn't quite the same*. This difference is hard to verbalize since it's beyond the mental realm. But there's a subtle change in your perception.

When you're in embodied awakening, your higher self is driving. This means your higher self is operating your human self. That's how this state is possible.

An unawakened human can't be consistently free of thoughts and challenging emotions without effort. But once your higher self has merged with you, it's effortless. It's your higher self's *natural state* to have no thoughts and no challenging emotions.

Partial Awakening

What if you don't meet all the criteria for embodied awakening, or some aren't at 100 percent?

Fortunately, awakening isn't an on-off switch. It's more like a dimmer control. *There are infinite gradations between spiritual unconsciousness and enlightenment.*

For example, here's Amanda's story of partial awakening:

> A friend told me that Benjamin's invocations had helped her enormously. I had just been divorced and was homeless. My life was quite scattered. I meditate a lot, but I wasn't able to concentrate for more than a few minutes without my monkey mind going around and around and around!
>
> Even when I wasn't meditating, I was procrastinating a lot. And I was experiencing lots of mental interruptions and constant mind chatter throughout the day.
>
> So, I started doing Benjamin's invocations. It took about a week before I felt a little more calm. There was still some mind chatter, but it was settling down enormously. I felt a lot more peaceful.
>
> — Amanda Elwell

Congratulate yourself for *any* progress toward the effortless experience of peacefulness with no mental chatter or challenging emotions. Even baby steps are worth celebrating!

I've worked with people who couldn't lock into embodied awakening at first. Happily, many ultimately achieved it when they persisted.

Once you attain embodied awakening, soak in this blissful state as long as you like. You deserve it!

Before we get to the bare-bones instructions for the Embodied Awakening Invocation, let's hear Emily's inspiring story:

> I remember the first time I used Benjamin's invocations. I

had left a long-term relationship. I had also left a career and was coming down off the high of those changes. In my new reality, I felt unsure of what I was doing and where my life was heading.

I had to do so much learning around who I was. Who did I want to become? I was struggling with a lot of anxiety. I was looking externally for signs of what I should do — as if that knowledge existed outside of me!

I was working so hard with shadow work and therapy. But I was struggling and felt really lost.

Then, one morning, **I did the Embodied Awakening Invocation for the first time. I felt this immense peace come over me. It felt like total Presence.** It was the opposite of the anxious distraction I'd been struggling with.

I had experienced that feeling before, in deeply spiritual moments. And I had always struggled and failed to get back to it.

But now I realized that, *with the Embodied Awakening Invocation, I could just tap into Presence whenever I wished. And in such a simple way!* That was quite profound for me.

I still use the invocations when I start to spin out, to get back into that peaceful state. Sometimes I'll use the invocation to bring me back into the present moment — into what is most true and authentic.

With the invocations, I can put my higher self in the driver's seat. Being able to do that without needing anything external is really empowering.

— Emily

Bare-Bones Instructions for the Embodied Awakening Invocation

Say, **"Maximum embodied awakening that serves highest good, please."**

If you feel subtle energy moving in your body, hold passive awareness of it during the invocation process. Otherwise, hold passive awareness of your breath coming and going on its own.

While the invocation fills you with energy...

> Don't make anything happen by using effort or willpower.
>
> Don't *stop* anything from happening.
>
> Don't *deliberately* visualize or imagine anything.

If a distraction arises,

> Don't fight it.
>
> Don't try to change it.
>
> Let it be exactly as it is, with no resistance.

After noting a distraction, relax back into subtle energy or breath.

Use the least possible effort that keeps your focus on subtle energy or breath.

When you're in embodied awakening, four things will be true at the same time:

1. No mental chatter.

2. No challenging emotion.

3. You'll feel peaceful.

4. All this will be completely effortless.

As a reminder, Key Takeaways for Chapters Two through Eleven are in Appendix B. These could give you the essential information you need when you return to this book, and could eliminate the need to reread an entire chapter.

There are two foundational IDA Invocations. You just learned the one for embodied awakening. Now it's time to learn how to delegate your healing to your higher self!

CHAPTER THREE: THE HEALING INVOCATION

Woody and Buzz Lightyear. Captain Kirk and Mr. Spock. Laurel and Hardy. What do they have in common with the Healing Invocation and the Embodied Awakening Invocation?

They're natural partners.

You just learned how Emily uses the Embodied Awakening Invocation to stay peaceful. She also had this potent experience with the Healing Invocation:

> I had a really, really painful breakup a few months ago. It ripped open all sorts of old wounds. It was excruciating — a lot more emotional pain than I've had to deal with in a long time.
>
> I was doing all the conceptual, intellectual work around what happened. But there was also spiritual and emotional pain that I didn't know what to do with.
>
> Then I used the Healing Invocation and felt this pain open up in my chest. I felt immense relief and started crying. I felt the pain just melt out of me.

It was so helpful to process the pain from that breakup. **It was so empowering to know that my higher self and I could heal it. I didn't need anything external. I didn't need to pay for anything. I didn't need to talk to any other human. It all happened within me.**

At first, I was so surprised that these invocations worked. It makes me wonder what other amazing possibilities that I can't even imagine might open to me as I keep using them!

— Emily

The Great Onion of Consciousness

How did the Healing Invocation help Emily release so much emotional pain? And how can it help you heal... more quickly and easily than you might have thought possible?

To answer this, let's explore the *Great Onion of Consciousness*.

A Tangent of Gratitude

But first, it's time for a quick tangent. I want to give *more* credit where it's due.

I'm deeply grateful to my plant spirit teachers for opening these inner worlds to me. These magnificent beings of love and light include ayahuasca, San Pedro, magic mushrooms, and Grandfather Tobacco. I'm also grateful to the shamans and medicine carriers who facilitated the plant spirit ceremonies I attended.

I also offer profound thanks to my other allies of high vibration and benevolent intent. These include ascended masters, deities from many religions, sacred apus (mountain spirits), and power animals.

It's only through the extraordinary grace and generosity of these divine allies that I can offer you the information in this book. At the human level, I can only strive to be a worthy conduit for their love, power, and guidance.

Tangent complete. Let's get back to that onion!

How the Great Onion Relates to Your Human and Higher Selves

Here's a basic explanation of the Great Onion of Consciousness.

Your higher self is a deeply awakened being of love and light. At just the right moment, part of it came down to earth and animated your human body. The rest of it stayed in the spirit realm. From there, it watches your progress and occasionally drops hints we call "intuition."

Your human self had to go "behind the veil" to experience this incarnation. For your human experience to serve its function, you needed at least some spiritual amnesia. (A few rare souls don't get this forgetfulness, but you'd know if you were one of these exceptions.)

Your human self bumbles through life the best it can. It uses the limited tools available to it in the physical realm... until you start awakening. Then you get to use vastly superior methods!

Your higher self deliberately brought certain past-life wounds and traumas into this lifetime. This gives you a chance to heal them once and for all! It also brought in many gifts and talents.

Your higher self — the soul that you *really* are — is awesome beyond words. From your human perspective, your higher self's everyday reality is full of ecstasy, bliss, and euphoria.

Circling Back

Here's how all this relates to the Great Onion. Every unhealed wound or trauma puts a dark layer around your higher self's luminous core. These traumas might be from this life or a previous one.

These layers build up until your soul looks like an onion. The bright ecstatic core of your higher self is at the center, surrounded by dark layers of unhealed pain.

This onion exists in the spiritual dimension. You can imagine your human self below it on the physical plane.

Some of that divine light shines through the onion. But the dark layers of pain block the rest.

Peeling the Onion Layers

The magic of the Healing Invocation is that it peels these layers one by one. Every time a layer peels off, the light seems brighter to your human self. This is because there's less heavy energy blocking it.

Even peeling one layer can open you to a profound new level of euphoria. Just one good healing round can bless you with a magnificent altered state. It's as if you took some amazing drug, and the side effects are all positive!

That's the basic idea behind the Healing Invocation. Your ego calls in healing from your higher self. Then your higher self does the healing for you, while your human self passively receives it.

Pam's Physical Healing

In this chapter's opening story, you learned how Emily used the Healing Invocation to eliminate her emotional pain. But the Healing Invocation can also give permanent *physical* healing, as shown in Pam's story:

> I've been using Benjamin's invocations for over two years and have had amazing results. I've had some very deep healing experiences with repressed material. This has sparked deep releases of misalignment in my body.
>
> The most recent one involved mother issues in my left hip, leg, and ankle. I've always been a very active person and love hiking. I was still doing it but it wasn't comfortable.
>
> My left hip had been hurting off and on for about six months. I only go to alternative healers, not medical doctors. I had gone to a regular chiropractor a couple of days before but he didn't relieve the pain. I really like Network Chiropractic but that wasn't available. Yoga stretches and poses didn't help either.
>
> All this was very disappointing and I was in a quandary. So, I finally did the Healing Invocation.
>
> And did it ever work! There was no question that it was realigning my hip because the pain was so strong. And this intense healing process must have lasted for an hour!
>
> But I felt cleared at the end and I've never had another issue with my hip. It was one-hundred percent healed!

So, I got what I wanted and it was totally worth the pain. It was amazing how my hip, leg, and ankle were back in perfect alignment after the session!

I've done a lot of different self-healing modalities. But out of all the healings I've done on myself over the years, Benjamin's Healing Invocation is the topper.

— Pam Chapman

I'll chime in after Pam. The Healing Invocation remains my go-to technique for healing challenges within myself. I've used it more times than I can count over the years. And the more I use it the more effective it becomes!

How to Do the Healing Invocation

Let's do the Healing Invocation now.

Most people find the Healing Invocation easier at first when my voice guides them. You get the instructions without having to read them, and the recording transmits healing frequencies to help you.

Go to InstantDivineAssistance.com for a free recording of me guiding you through this process step by step.

As in the previous chapter, step-by-step instructions follow, supplemented with helpful information. You'll find bare-bones instructions at the end of this chapter.

Close your eyes as much as possible, for the same reasons I gave in Chapter Two.

If possible, do this when you're in embodied awakening. Invoke embodied awakening first if needed. This speeds up the healing process, and you'll probably save time overall.

There may be times when you can't get into embodied awakening before you do the Healing Invocation. If so, no worries. Just do the Healing Invocation on its own.

For starters, notice anything that doesn't feel wonderful. It could be physical, emotional, or both. You'll use this as your focus.

How to Proactively Heal a Past Trauma

What if you can't find a physical or emotional challenge? You can do a variation of the Healing Invocation. To do this, deliberately bring up a past trauma.

This needs to be something painful from your past. Remembering it needs to bring up challenging feelings.

You'll Never Feel Overwhelmed

Let me jump in with some reassurance. One wonderful thing about the Healing Invocation, if done as described in this book, is that *you'll never feel overwhelmed*. You could be working on the worst trauma you've ever experienced — a 10 out of 10 — and still be safe.

How can I make such a bold claim? Because your higher self will watch you like a hawk the entire time. It will only bring up the amount of challenging energy you can process at that moment.

Your higher self is no fool. It knows that if you feel overwhelmed *even once* when doing this process, you might never do it again.

So, it will never let that happen. If a major trauma needs more than one round to process, it will spread it over as many rounds as necessary.

I speak from experience. *In eleven years of facilitating the Healing Invocation, I've never had a single person report overwhelm.*

So — say it with me — **you absolutely, positively don't have to worry about overwhelm!**

If you're recalling a past trauma, visualize it happening right now. Imagine it as vividly as you can.

At this point, you'll be at the same stage in the Healing Invocation process as if something was already bothering you. From here forward, it doesn't matter whether something was already disturbing you or if you called up a past trauma. The instructions are the same either way.

Focus on the Feeling

You should now feel challenging energy in your body. Even emotional challenge will have a physical location. Notice where it's strongest.

Sometimes the challenging feeling has a central point where it's strongest. If so, put your attention on this point.

Sometimes the challenging feeling is more broadly and evenly distributed. In that case put your attention on all of it at once.

Next, give this challenging feeling a number. Use a zero-to-10 intensity scale. Ten is as strong as it could possibly be. Zero is no challenge at all.

What number is it right now?

*Note: Doctors use a zero-to-10 **pain** scale. But "pain" might not describe what you feel. That's why I have you use an intensity scale, which works for any sensation.*

Ignore All Thoughts and Images

The following instruction is crucial to doing the Healing Invocation successfully. It's also different from many other healing approaches and might surprise you.

Don't concern yourself with what the challenge is or why it's happening. Don't get into a story about it. Mental activity won't help you when doing this invocation. It will only interfere.

Once the Healing Invocation has run its course, you can think to your mind's content. But while you're in the process, *ignore all thoughts*. For our purposes, all thoughts are distractions. Focus on what you *feel*.

The same goes for images. It's common for thoughts and images to swirl around while you're doing the Healing Invocation. That's fine. Let them swirl. Just don't focus on them.

Put your attention on what you're feeling. Keep coming back to pure sensation if you get distracted. We all get distracted, and there's nothing wrong with it. But the Healing Invocation will work best if you just keep returning attention to what you *feel*.

So here you are, feeling that challenging sensation. You've given it an intensity number from zero to 10.

Now it's time to call your higher self to take care of this. Say the following, out loud if you can, silently if you must:

"Maximum healing that serves highest good, please."

Let the words go. Rest your attention on the challenging sensation. Focus on the central point of intensity if it has one, or more broadly if it doesn't. Let the thoughts and images swirl but keep returning your attention to pure sensation.

How to Zero In on Minimum Effort

In the Embodied Awakening Invocation, you used the minimum effort that got the job done. This is effective for all IDA Invocations, so we'll do something similar here.

Drop to zero effort. "Just be" for a moment. You'll probably lose at least some awareness of the discomfort.

Then gradually add teeny-tiny bits of effort to help you regain full awareness of the discomfort. Keep adding micro-increments of effort, until adding effort gives you no extra awareness of it.

Now, fine-tune your effort level. Reduce it until you start to *lose* awareness of the challenging sensation. Then gradually increase your effort until it's a bit more than you need.

Go back and forth like this a time or two, until you feel the sweet spot. This is where you're using *barely enough* effort to feel the challenging sensation completely.

Now just relax into that level. You might be surprised how little effort this is!

As you rest your attention on simple somatic awareness, right where the challenge is, you shine a spotlight there. It's like saying to your higher self, "*This* is where I need healing." You simply hold awareness there, while your higher self takes care of everything.

Your healing may happen rapidly or may take a while. Either way, you can be sure your higher self is working as fast as it can. It always does!

How to Release or Transmute Heavy Energy

Your higher self will clear or transmute the challenging energy as quickly as it can without overwhelming you. As I've already emphasized so strongly, it will *never* give you more than you can handle.

In most cases, your higher self will flush heavy energy from your body. The most common exit routes are through your hands and feet.

It's helpful to have your body positioned so that the heavy energy can exit most easily. If your legs are extended, it's best not to cross your ankles. (Crossed ankles are fine if you're sitting Indian-style.)

I also recommend that you don't cross your arms, clasp your hands, or use mudras (hand positions) that stop energy from exiting your hands. If you're laying down, consider having your hands by your sides instead of on your body.

None of these suggestions is mandatory. But they will make it easier for heavy energy to leave your body.

When you release heavy energy, your process might be smooth and easy. Your body might stay still and silent.

Or your experience might be more dramatic. Your body might shake or tremble. (Sometimes I feel like a human vibrator!)

You might sob, wail, shout, or scream. Tears might stream down your face. You might be inspired to stand up and stomp, flail your arms, or move your body in all kinds of different ways.

Don't be a drama queen for the hell of it. But do let your body release heavy energy however it wants to.

It's okay to be a hot mess for a while. Just do it as consciously as you can!

Let this heavy energy flow into Mother Earth. It may sound strange, but she's *delighted* to receive your heavy energy! So, release it to Mother Earth without hesitation. You could even think of it as a sacred offering.

Other things might also happen to this heavy energy. It might radiate out in concentric circles. Sometimes it stays and transmutes from dark to light. In this case, the transformed energy stays to empower you.

Here's a wonderful thing about the Healing Invocation: your human self doesn't have to decide what happens. Everything runs on autopilot. Your ego's only job is to hold awareness on the challenging sensation. If your mind wanders, simply refocus.

Chellenging Energy: When To Track Or Shift

Sometimes, the point of discomfort stays in the same place. But sometimes it moves around. If so, track it like a hound dog! Stay with it until it fades away or completely leaves your energy field.

Sometimes, when doing the Healing Invocation, you'll feel challenging energy getting strong somewhere else in your body.

If so, it's okay to shift your attention there.

Hold your attention wherever the challenging energy is strongest. It's helpful to note the intensity number (zero through 10) of the point you're shifting to. This lets you consciously track your healing process.

Holding attention on one point at a time is best for most people. But some people can hold attention on two or more points. If this is easy for you, and speeds up the healing process, feel free to hold attention on multiple points of challenging energy.

After you say the Healing Invocation and focus on the challenging energy, you'll obviously be feeling unpleasant sensations. But you have to feel it to heal it. (Fortunately, you'll never experience overwhelm. Did I mention that yet?)

From Challenge to Euphoria

After a while, something nice starts to happen. For the most part, you'll still feel challenged. But you'll start noticing a pleasant feeling around the edges of your energy field. The challenging energy will gradually decrease, while the pleasant energy blossoms.

Eventually, the pleasure will outweigh the challenge. Most people who let a healing round run its full course end up with no discomfort and lots of euphoria!

At this point your physical body may feel more like energy than solid matter. Mystics and physicists know the universe is really made of energy. Solid matter is an illusion. Now you get to experience this firsthand.

You'll have this experience because the Healing Invocation shifts your perception. It has peeled a layer of the Great Onion of Consciousness. And this has taken you a step deeper into spiritual awakening.

Are you experiencing a pleasant feeling and don't feel any more heavy energy being processed? Then that healing round is complete. Chances are that your discomfort is gone, or significantly decreased. If the challenge is completely gone, go on about your business.

When to Do More Healing Rounds

If some discomfort remains, and you have a bit more time, it's best to do another healing round. Additional rounds usually go much faster than the first one. I've witnessed many Healing Invocations where the first round took ten or fifteen minutes, but additional rounds only took a minute or two!

Check Your Work

Did you do the version of the Healing Invocation where you deliberately called up a past trauma? If so, it's always good to "check your work" at the end.

To do this, once again recall the trauma you chose to work with. Remember it as vividly as you can.

Now, note your emotional response. Rate it on the zero to 10 intensity scale.

I've frequently worked with clients who initially felt the trauma they chose as a nine or 10 when they started this process. But, after they did one Healing Invocation round and checked their work, it had usually dropped to zero. If they reported it as a one or two after the first round, it usually dropped to zero after the second round.

At first, I found it hard to believe that a major trauma which had caused so much suffering, sometimes for decades, could be healed in a matter of minutes. But, after seeing it happen so often, I got used to it. Never underestimate the healing power of your higher self!

Does checking your work and getting a zero absolutely guarantee that you've cleared every last trace of that trauma?

Not necessarily. As you'll learn near the end of Chapter Four, you can't know what's buried in your unconscious mind. There might be another layer of that trauma waiting to come up for healing once you've cleared the part you know about.

If so, no worries. It will be no match for the Healing Invocation!

Challenges That Can't Heal

I've seen the Healing Invocation work lots of miracles, but they aren't guaranteed. This is because some things can heal… and some can't.

This may be the last thing you want to hear! But I believe some souls choose to take on a specific challenge before they incarnate… and the deal is non-negotiable. It's a lifetime contract.

This is an essential part of their soul evolution. They must learn to gracefully accept and adapt to this situation.

Stephen Hawking's Soul Choice

For example, I believe that Stephen Hawking's soul deliberately planned for him to spend most of his life as a paraplegic. This was because Hawking came to bring the world a major breakthrough in physics, and to open people's minds with books like *A Brief History of Time*.

He couldn't afford to get distracted from his mission. So, his soul ruled out the possibility of most distractions by taking away his physical mobility.

Hawking worked within his extreme limitations to excel at his mission. His heroic example also inspired differently-abled people and helped the world see them more positively.

Of course, you shouldn't meekly accept every difficulty as a permanent condition. It's always worth trying the Healing Invocation to see if it can clear a particular challenge.

Anjuli's Healing Story

That's what Anjuli did when her life went off the rails. We'll close Chapter Three with her story:

> I've been lucky enough to work with Benjamin's invocations for about eight years now. They've helped me through a lot of life situations.
>
> When I first started working with the invocations, I had just come out of a very abusive relationship. I was struggling to love myself. I was struggling with anxiety and emotional pain. My entire life was in upheaval.
>
> Getting grounded was extremely hard. But the invocations, as I kept using them, became a touchstone to help me find my center. They helped me reduce the intensity of my emotions, stress, and pain.

I've been through some big life events since, including a car accident, and the invocations have been an anchor for me. They're so helpful in every possible situation!

The invocations keep me calm on the daily level. But they really help me when I face something major — when I hit something really big that feels so overwhelming. It could be the car accident, a loss in the family, or when I feel out of control inside… when I'm bursting with emotions, vulnerability or anxiety.

All that flushes out with the invocations. I feel clear-headed. The physical stress releases.

I end up getting this wash through my whole Spirit. My mind, emotions and physical body become calm. The invocations help me face whatever I'm going through with more grace.

Everything is improved, from my sleep to my ability to deal with additional stresses or changes. It has this overall calming effect and, at the same time, it's extremely empowering!

— Anjuli

Bare-Bones Instructions for the Healing Invocation

Say (or think) the Healing Invocation: **"Maximum healing that serves highest good, please."**

Let the words go and rest your attention on the challenging sensation.

Focus on the central point of intensity if it has one or focus more broadly if it doesn't.

Use the minimum effort that gives you complete awareness of the challenging feeling.

If heavy energy wants to exit your body, let it leave.

If heavy energy wants to transmute to love and light, let it.

If challenging energy moves around, track it like a hound dog until it completely leaves your energy field.

If energy that's more challenging arises elsewhere, you can shift your attention there.

If you can easily hold attention on more than one challenged area at a time, and this speeds up the healing, that's okay.

The challenging energy will gradually decrease, while euphoric energy increases.

Eventually, the euphoria will outweigh the challenge.

If you let a healing round run its full course, you'll usually feel abundant euphoria and no discomfort. Your physical body may feel more like energy than solid matter.

Are you experiencing euphoria and don't feel any more heavy energy being processed? Then that healing round is complete. Chances are that your discomfort is either gone or significantly reduced.

If your challenge is completely gone, go on about your business.

If some discomfort remains, and you have a bit more time,

it's best to do another healing round. Extra rounds usually go much faster than the first one.

Some things can heal, while others can't. The Healing Invocation is always worth a try, to see if it can clear a particular challenge.

So far, we've covered two ways to use the Healing Invocation. You can use it with a challenge that you feel right now, or to heal a past trauma.

In Chapter Five, you'll learn two more powerful ways to use the Healing Invocation. But next, you'll learn how to integrate the invocations for healing and awakening into a life-transforming daily practice!

CHAPTER FOUR: IDA INVOCATION DAILY MAINTENANCE

You've learned the basics of the Embodied Awakening Invocation and the Healing Invocation. Now you'll learn how to work with these two foundational Instant Divine Assistance Invocations daily. This will help you stabilize your embodied awakening... and keep taking it deeper!

Embodied awakening is so wonderful. Why settle for anything less? Why not live in this extraordinary awareness *every moment?*

This may sound like a fantasy, but it's not. I know because I've been living in embodied awakening for years. I can no longer tell where Benjamin ends and my higher self begins.

But embodied awakening is too good to keep to myself. I want you to enjoy it too!

So now, you'll learn how to maintain embodied awakening all day, every day. You'll also learn how and when to use the Healing Invocation.

I'm not saying these invocations are the all-time best DIY techniques for healing and awakening. They're just the best ones *I* know! Always use a different technique if it works better for you.

Are these invocations *your* best techniques for self-healing or self-awakening right now? Or are you trying them out? Then I encourage you to try the following daily practice.

Start Every Day with Embodied Awakening

First thing each morning, do the Embodied Awakening Invocation. Again, its eight words are:

"Maximum embodied awakening that serves highest good, please."

As described in Chapter Two, passively feel subtle energy or breath until your higher self merges with your human self. Then ask yourself the confirmation question. Is there peacefulness, no mental chatter, and no challenging emotion… all with no effort? If so, get on with your day.

Many people tell me they can invoke embodied awakening and have it lock in within five or ten seconds. Some people receive it before they even finish saying the eight words!

You might be used to meditating for a certain amount of time. But the IDA Invocations don't need a minimum duration. They aren't meditations. They're *invocations*, designed for maximum speed and efficiency.

You don't have to be at your altar or mesa. You could be lying in bed, sitting on the toilet, or standing on your head. Where you are, or what position your body is in, doesn't matter. Do it as soon as you think about it each day. Get your awakening on first thing!

Repeat as Needed

If your embodied awakening slips during the day, simply do the invocation again. **Repeat it as needed, *not* on a fixed schedule.**

You might just do it once in the morning, then stay in embodied awakening all day. If so, once is enough that day.

Or maybe you're having a hard day. Mental chatter and challenging emotions keep coming back. If so, you might need to refresh your awakening dozens of times! Just take each day as it comes.

It's best to say the words out loud. Audible sound creates extra power.

But don't let the perfect be the enemy of the good. The IDA Invocations will work just fine if you do them silently. Thoughts are also powerful!

You can even do these invocations in full view of other people. Most won't have a clue you're doing anything unusual. (If someone has psychic sight, they'll probably be impressed!)

So, you don't even have to wait until you're alone. **You can do the IDA Invocations anytime, anywhere, anyplace.**

If you lose your embodied awakening, I strongly recommend refreshing it right away. You don't want to risk falling into amnesia! (You'll learn how to avoid the dangers of spiritual amnesia in Chapter Eight.)

When to Use the Healing Invocation

When would you use the Healing Invocation? When the Embodied Awakening Invocation doesn't stop your mental chatter or challenging emotions, or if you want deeper healing. And the sooner the better!

Whoever or whatever triggered you actually did you a favor. A layer of your Great Onion of Consciousness had been thick and calcified. Then this challenging catalyst liquefied it. Now, it's bubbling hot and ready to release.

All you have to do is call in your higher self to finish the job. You could even thank the catalyst for getting the heavy energy roiled up!

Once you're triggered, invoke the Healing Invocation as soon as possible. The longer you wait, the more the heavy energy will solidify again. It will be thicker and harder to work with. That's why sooner is better.

You can do the Healing Invocation with whatever time you have available. Your higher self will process as much heavy energy as it can.

Do you only have a moment? It's still worth doing. Process as much heavy energy as time permits. You can always do another healing round later to clear the rest.

That Pain Is Gone Forever!

Here's one of the most amazing things about the Healing Invocation. Any layer of heavy energy that you flush or transmute is *gone, once and for all!*

There are lots of techniques that claim to heal you. But many are like Band-Aids. These temporary fixes might give you a break from a challenging situation. But the pain will always return... until you use a truly effective healing method.

With the Healing Invocation, your higher self can pull out the spiritual root of a challenge. Once it does, the symptoms — physical, emotional, and mental — will automatically fall away. A weed always dies after the root is pulled.

This doesn't mean you'll never feel a similar discomfort. Sometimes there are several onion layers that feel comparable. But if a similar challenge returns, it should become less intense with each layer.

Your unconscious mind can also factor into this. Trauma that you aren't yet ready to process is stored here, out of your conscious awareness. Sometimes, once you fully clear a challenge you know about, a related trauma that was "waiting in the wings" can finally come up for healing.

This can be temporarily challenging, but ultimately it's a blessing. You can use the Healing Invocation to clear it quickly and efficiently. And every onion layer you peel strengthens the euphoria of your embodied awakening!

So, that's how to use these two invocations as partners. To summarize:

> **First thing each morning, do the Embodied Awakening Invocation. Say, "Maximum embodied awakening that serves highest good, please." Repeat as needed throughout the day.**
>
> **When you get triggered more strongly, use the Healing Invocation: "Maximum healing that serves highest good, please."**

These two techniques can radically improve your life. If you haven't locked in embodied awakening yet, you can upgrade to an extraordinary new level of consciousness. If your awakening is already consistent, the IDA Invocations can take you deeper. Either way, everything about your life can become more wonderful!

Remember when I said there were two more ways to use the Healing Invocation? That's what you'll learn in the next chapter!

CHAPTER FIVE: FOUR WAYS TO USE THE HEALING INVOCATION

I've discovered four different ways to use the Healing Invocation so far. You've already learned two of them. Now, it's time to learn the others!

Brief Review of the First Two Methods

First, let's briefly review the first two methods. You might use the Healing Invocation most often when you're already stirred up. You want to get rid of challenging emotions or physical discomfort that are already bothering you. Say, **"Maximum healing that serves highest good, please."** Then passively feel the challenging phenomenon while your higher self heals it for you.

You've also learned a second way to use the Healing Invocation: deliberately bring up an old trauma from your past. Once you feel its challenging energy, ask your higher self to heal it for you.

The Third Method: Next in Line!

Here's a third way to use the Healing Invocation: healing whatever's next in line.

Let's say you're feeling perfectly fine, with no challenging emotions or physical discomfort. But you want to speed up your awakening process.

You understand the Great Onion of Consciousness, and know your awakening is already there waiting for you. You just have to peel the dark layers blocking your deeper enlightenment.

There's just one problem. *You may have no idea what specific traumas those onion layers contain. How can you peel a layer if you don't know what challenge created it?*

"Ignorance Is Bliss" Healing

Here's some great news: you don't have to know!

This is one of the most extraordinary things about the Healing Invocation. It's also something which, at first, can be so hard to believe.

You can completely heal trauma without knowing anything about it.

Yes, I know how crazy that sounds. It flies in the face of conventional psychological wisdom.

I also would have thought this idea was crazy — if I hadn't experienced it dozens of times myself. And if I hadn't witnessed hundreds of my clients and "Awakening Plus" members having major permanent healings... with no idea what they were releasing!

Fortunately, it's easy to do this. Just say to your higher self, **"Maximum healing that serves highest good, please."**

Give your higher self a moment to bring up whatever heavy energy is next in line. Once you notice a challenging sensation, passively rest your attention there. Then let the Healing Invocation play itself out, as described in Chapter Three.

That's all there is to it!

"I Don't Want to Miss the Lesson"

There's a question that sometimes comes up when people learn the Healing Invocation. It might be in your mind too, so let's address it.

Here's the question:

*"If I clear a challenge energetically but don't know what it is, won't I miss the lesson I need to learn from it? And if I don't learn the lesson, won't the challenge repeat until I **do** learn it?"*

First, let's question the assumption that intellectual understanding is the best path to healing.

How many people do you know who've spent years in therapy? They've gained a deep intellectual understanding of their psychological challenges — but still suffer from them. This scenario is tragically common and suggests that *a mental approach to healing may not always be the most effective.*

Other Experiential Therapies

Earlier, I said, "You have to feel it to heal it." There's a reason experiential therapies are exploding in popularity. They include:

Holotropic Breathwork, Shamanic Breathwork, and other breathwork modalities

Somatic Experiencing

Ecstatic dance

Shamanic ceremonies, which might include psychoactive plant spirit teachers like ayahuasca, San Pedro, or magic mushrooms

Other psychedelic therapies

Internal Family Systems Therapy

Family Constellations

Compassionate Inquiry

Music therapy

EFT (Emotional Freedom Technique, aka "tapping")

Art therapy

Equine and animal-assisted therapy

Psychodrama

Adventure therapies, including wilderness therapy

Do You Have to Know What You're Healing?

All these healing modalities put you in touch with what you *feel*. Like the Healing Invocation, they can open the door to profound healings that don't require mental understanding.

I've facilitated hundreds of healing sessions in my ten years as a professional shamanic healer. I've seen successful healings go one of two ways:

> 1. The client has a powerful clearing or transmutation but doesn't know what they released.
>
> 2. The client has a powerful clearing or transmutation and has at least some awareness of the specific trauma being healed.

I've followed up with lots of these clients. But I've seen no evidence that those who knew what was being healed had better outcomes.

This has also been my personal experience. I've had plenty of healings in both categories and found both types equally effective.

I include the Healing Invocation in my daily spiritual practice. I routinely feel heavy energy release but rarely experience thoughts or emotions with it. Nevertheless, I'm significantly more light and clear afterward.

You Can't Fully Understand Divine Energy... So Just Enjoy It!

I have a similar experience when I call in highest good energy during my daily spiritual practice. I can feel euphoric divine energy pouring in through my crown chakra and saturating my body. But thoughts or images rarely appear.

I'm given spiritual information only on a need-to-know basis. That's just fine with me. I'm burning more than enough mental calories already!

I prefer this need-to-know arrangement. In spiritual matters, excessive curiosity can be a hindrance. As you learned earlier, a level can't comprehend a level beyond itself. And the spiritual levels exist beyond the mental plane.

My intellect beat its head against the wall for years, trying in vain to understand the spiritual levels. But it was like a two-year-old trying to understand particle physics. It just wasn't going to happen!

When my intellect finally accepted this, I became much happier. Once my ego humbly accepted the limits of its cognition, it was a great relief.

That Which I Am has a wonderful time merging and serving in these higher levels of consciousness. And it's delighted to share as much of this exquisite energy with my human self as serves highest good. But my human part has wisely abandoned its pointless attempts to intellectually comprehend this energy and consciousness.

A Final Thought on "Missing the Lesson"

Let's wrap up this "Missing the Lesson" discussion by revisiting the question that started it:

"If I clear a challenge energetically but don't know what it is, won't I miss the lesson it was trying to teach me? And if I don't learn the

*lesson, won't the challenge repeat until I **do** learn it?"*

This question might have a false premise. Based on my experience, there isn't always a lesson associated with every healing experience. So, there's no need to worry about missing important lessons when you do the Healing Invocation.

Your higher self is one smart cookie. If there's something your ego needs to know during a healing round, your higher self will give it all the thoughts or images it needs. And you can work with those all you want... *after* the healing round is over!

If no thoughts or images pop in, that's even better. You save time and energy by not having to do any mental processing. Ignorance is bliss!

The Thought-Focused Healing Invocation

Now, let's learn the fourth variation on the Healing Invocation.

But get ready for a surprise. This variation contradicts one of the cardinal rules of the IDA Invocations. Instead of ignoring thought, this invocation puts it front and center!

What? Didn't I tell you to treat all thoughts as distractions? Aren't thoughts the uninvited guests you're supposed to ignore?

I held this as gospel truth... until I worked with clients whose relentless mental chatter wouldn't stop for *anything!* The other versions of the Healing Invocation didn't clear it, so I came up with this variation. It usually clears mental chatter — even for clients who had lost hope of ever quieting their minds.

Here's how to do the **Thought-Focused Healing Invocation**.

The Two-Story Thought House

Imagine you're in a two-story house. You're with your thoughts on the ground floor, and they're yammering away as usual.

You walk up the stairs to the second floor. Then you walk over to a balcony, which gives you a clear view of the thoughts on the first floor.

Give the chattering thoughts your full attention. Then say the Healing Invocation as usual: **"Maximum healing that serves highest good, please."**

Notice that you're a level up from the thoughts. You're not thinking them. They're operating under their own power, completely apart from you.

You are pure awareness. You're simply witnessing what the thoughts are doing on their own.

René Descartes was wrong when he famously declared, "I think, therefore I am." It would be more correct to say, "I *have consciousness*, therefore I am."

This process lets you experience thoughts as independent entities. A thought is a little energy being who wants a host — you! — so it can gain power.

Thoughts Are Like Viruses

Thoughts are like viruses. A virus is a partial life form. It only comes fully alive when it draws on another being's energy. Without a host, a thought can't grow to maximum strength and breed more thought-forms.

Like viruses, there's a huge number of thought-forms floating around the Earth. And they all want a human host!

This means *you don't actually have your own thoughts*. You are pure consciousness. But you have *a community of thought-forms* that hang around and help you think… just as you have gut bacteria that help you digest your food.

If you've done the Embodied Awakening Invocation successfully, you're in a state of pure awareness. There isn't a thought in sight. You're just consciousness, pure and simple. No thoughts are needed for you to exist!

That's why, when doing the Thought-Focused Healing Invocation, you can be a level up from those chattering thoughts. You can look down and simply observe them. When you do this, the thoughts are powerless to seduce you with their mental temptations.

Many meditation practices use a similar metaphor. You imagine that you're sitting on a riverbank, with the thoughts floating by. You're not the thoughts, you're just watching them.

The house metaphor is similar. You're on the second floor, and the thoughts are on the ground floor.

What happens as you simply observe thoughts, rather than engage with them? They slow down. Then they stop. Finally, they dissolve.

Good-bye, mental chatter. Hello, uncluttered mind!

So, that's the fourth variation on the Healing Invocation. And the final one so far.

Ayahuasca's Thought-Form Lesson

Years ago, in one of my ayahuasca ceremonies, the medicine gave me a vivid teaching on thought-forms. I saw my thoughts as protoplasmic beings. They would form in my brain, wriggle out the front of my head, and float into the physical world.

As I watched this with my inner sight, ayahuasca told me that every thought a person thinks generates these thought-forms. Each thought-form will do its best to *physically manifest* the thought it carries. If I'd spoken the thought, the medicine said, the thought-forms would have been a hundred times more potent!

I already believed that thoughts create reality. But it was fascinating to observe how the process starts in the inner dimensions.

Each person's dominant thoughts powerfully influence their personal reality. This happens whether the thoughts are consciously generated or running in the background. If your autopilot thoughts don't support the reality you want, the Two-Story Thought House visualization can help you dissolve them!

Summary of the Four Healing Invocation Methods

Let's summarize the four ways you can use the Healing Invocation:

> 1. You get triggered by something and experience a challenging physical or emotional sensation. You say, **"Maximum healing that serves highest good, please."** Then you gently focus on the challenging feeling while your higher self heals it for you.

2. You deliberately remember an unhealed trauma to get it stirred up. Then you say the Healing Invocation and focus as described above. You can systematically heal your old traumas by doing this.

3. Say the Healing Invocation, then let your higher self bring up the next trauma in line to be healed. Wait until you feel a challenge arise, then focus on it and follow the usual procedure.

4. To eliminate unrelenting thoughts, use the Healing Invocation with the Two-Story Thought House visualization.

If you come up with your own Healing Invocation variation, please email it to me at benjamin@astroshaman.com. I'd love to consider it for a future version of this book!

Can You Multitask the Healing Invocation?

This section gets a bit technical. You can skip it if you wish.

So far, everything you've learned about the Healing Invocation has assumed that you're focusing on one issue at a time.

But what if you want to multitask? Can you do a Healing Invocation for two or more challenges at the same time? If so, would they all have to be in the same category (physical, emotional, mental, or spiritual)? Or could you invoke healing in multiple categories at the same time?

When you first start working with the Healing Invocation, I definitely recommend focusing on one thing at a time. If that's all you ever did, you could still have wonderful outcomes.

After you gain some experience, you might want to try the Healing Invocation on more than one challenge at a time. But, as you've learned, the Healing Invocation only works if you hold your attention on the area being healed.

It would be simplest to start with one area of the body that has multiple challenges. Let's say that someone had both anger issues and digestive problems. Anger issues would probably be focused in the third chakra, which is located behind the solar plexus. And the solar plexus is near the stomach and intestines.

These challenges are in different categories: emotional and physical. But you could call your higher self to heal them at the same time, since you'd be focusing your attention on the same area of the body. This shouldn't be too hard, since you'd be ignoring thoughts and images and focusing entirely on physical sensations.

If you want to receive simultaneous healing in two or more areas of your body, you'd have to be able to hold your attention on all of them at once. Can you do this while also staying present with any challenging experiences that arise? If so, you might be able to do multiple healings in different parts of the body at the same time.

Spontaneous Simultaneous Healings

I've had many experiences where simultaneous healing in different parts of the body happened on its own. This usually happens when I invoke a normal Healing Invocation and just focus on a challenge in one part of the body. After a while, I'll notice that healing energy is working in two or more parts of my body at the same time.

Once I was aware of healing energy in five areas of my body

simultaneously! I had only asked for healing on one issue. But my higher self knew that all five areas needed work for the healing to succeed. Somehow, without even trying, I was able to hold awareness in all five areas at the same time.

So, the answer is: yes, it's possible to multitask the Healing Invocation. Or it might multitask itself!

Chloé's Story

We'll close Chapter Five with Chloé's story, which tells how the IDA Invocations helped her:

> Benjamin's invocations helped me when I was in a transitional stage on many levels.
>
> I had many challenges, but two were the hardest. First, I was confused about my career and how to communicate with my divine guidance. Second, I had a lot of challenging emotions because of all the transmutation and clearing I was experiencing.
>
> I didn't know what I should do with my life, although I knew deeply that something spiritual was awaiting me. And I could see that all these challenging emotions and situations were showing me an opportunity to evolve and release negative patterns.
>
> Sometimes I felt desperate. I felt a lot of doubt, sadness, anger, and loneliness.
>
> The invocations helped release patterns and stuck emotions that were ready to transmute — and they did it fast! They helped me get back in control of my inner peace and equanimity. They let me react in a "higher" way

so I could get in front of my challenges. And they helped me deepen my connection and communication with my divine guidance.

The main invocation I used was, *"Maximum divine awakening that serves highest good, please."* I also used many variations, such as:

"Maximum (joy / inner peace / unconditional love / divine neutrality / divine connection / abundance / divine inspiration / high vibrational state / etc.) that serves highest good, please."

Different invocations worked at different speeds. But to calm challenging emotions, they worked quickly and sometimes instantly.

I'm still on my learning path, but I have come a very long way! **Benjamin's invocations have helped my awakening and channeling abilities expand immensely.**

I can now officially call myself a channel. I quit my former career and am building a new one as a channel, energy healer, and writer. I'm more able to keep my cool in emotionally challenging situations. Finally, I'm able to contemplate my whole existence as a soul from a much higher perspective.

I'm so grateful to Benjamin's invocations for helping me do all this!

— Chloé

Chloe's story puts a strong focus on her healing journey. But she also mentions some variations, which let her invoke a variety of divine energies. You'll learn how to do this in Chapter Seven.

So far, you've learned several ways to use invocations for your own benefit. In the next chapter, you'll learn how to use the IDA Invocations to help others!

CHAPTER SIX: THE HOLLOW REED INVOCATION: HOW TO BE A CONDUIT FOR HIGHEST GOOD ENERGY

You've already learned the two essential Instant Divine Assistance Invocations. They're the Embodied Awakening Invocation and the Healing Invocation (along with its variations). These mainly help *you*.

Now, it's time to serve *others* with a third invocation. With this Hollow Reed Invocation, you can effortlessly flow highest good energy to anyone or anything!

As before, step-by-step instructions follow, supplemented with helpful information. The bare-bones instructions are at the end of this chapter.

As usual, close your eyes as much as possible while doing this. If you're not already in embodied awakening, invoke it if time allows. Being more awakened makes you a better conduit.

Take a moment to feel your body and the subtle energy in and around you. After you finish flowing energy to others, you'll compare how you feel before and after.

Now, decide where you want highest good energy to flow. It can be to one person, two or more people, or to one or more specific situations.

Actually, you can ask highest good energy to flow to anything you can imagine! But if you're just starting out, it's easiest to choose one person. I recommend starting with someone you love or like.

Say, **"Spirit that I am, please flow the energy through me to serve [name of the person(s) or situation(s)]'s highest good."**

After you say the words, let them go. If you feel energy flowing through you, passively feel what it's doing. If you don't feel this subtle energy, just feel your breath come and go on its own.

Just Be a Hollow Reed

The following instructions may seem strange at first. But the Hollow Reed Invocation will work much better if you follow them.

It's important that you **don't deliberately visualize anything**. Also, **don't use any effort to flow energy**.

Not only that, **you don't have to do anything with your hands**. When I flow energy to others, my hands are usually resting on my thighs, palms down.

You also don't need the permission of the person(s) receiving the energy. I'll tell you why not later in this chapter.

Your higher self uses your human self like a hollow reed. You're just a passive pipeline. Your motto for this invocation could be, "I conduit!" (Pun intended.)

If you're energetically sensitive, you may notice subtle energy flowing into your body through your crown chakra. (That's the energy center at the top of your head.) You may also feel energy flowing out the front of your body. It will pass through one or more of your chakras on its way to your recipient(s).

Simply notice this energy moving on its own. If you don't feel it, rest in passive breath awareness.

Did you invoke energy flow to another human? Then your higher self connects to their higher self and sends them a customized stream of energy. If you're sending to more than one person, it does this for each of them.

Your higher self can flow a huge number of energy streams at the same time. I've never found an upper limit. In fact, I routinely flow highest good energy to every being in the universe!

This Hollow Reed Invocation is so easy. Your human self is the passive witness, which takes almost no effort. Your higher self handles everything else!

What You *Don't* Have to Worry About

Here's what your human self *doesn't* have to worry about:

> What color is the energy?

> What spiritual plane(s) is the energy coming from?

> What other spiritual allies are helping flow the energy?

From your human perspective, all this runs on autopilot. That's because your higher self constantly monitors and adjusts the energy flow.

If time permits, let the energy flow until it stops on its own. But you can stop it whenever you like. Just say something like, "Let the energy flow stop now."

I usually get a physical signal when an energy flow has run its course: a brief, spontaneous head shake. Your higher self might also develop a customized "done" signal for you.

Don't expect a Hollow Reed energy flow to last a particular amount of time. Depending on the day, I've had the duration of an energy flow to the same destination vary significantly.

Over the years, I've also noticed that it takes less time to do an effective energy flow. The stronger your awakening becomes, the more fast and efficient your Hollow Reed Invocations will be.

A bigger, cleaner pipe delivers more water more quickly. Someday, you might be able to flow more helpful energy in five seconds than you could initially flow in five minutes!

Your Automatic Reward

Once the energy flow is complete, notice how your body and subtle energy feel. Compare this with how you felt before you invoked the energy flow.

Most people feel significantly *better* after this energy flow. This is because of a universal law: *what you give, you receive.*

Every time you flow highest good energy to others, you simultaneously receive highest good energy for yourself. This happens automatically. *One of the quickest ways to feel better is to invoke highest good energy for others!*

Over the years, some clients have told me they felt drained after flowing energy to someone. (They experienced this before working with me, and hadn't yet learned the Hollow Reed Invocation.)

When I asked about their technique for flowing energy, it usually involved visualization, willpower, and effort. Often, they were sending their *personal* energy to the other person. This could leave them feeling severely depleted.

Because of this negative experience, some clients were initially reluctant to try the Hollow Reed Invocation. Once burned, twice shy!

Eventually, I was able to help them understand how differently the Hollow Reed Invocation works. None of their personal energy would be drained. Doing it would require almost no effort. And, because they would automatically receive highest good energy for themselves as energy flowed to their recipient, they would probably end up with *more* vitality!

You Don't Have to Know What They Need

When you flow energy to others using this IDA Invocation, you don't have to know their highest good. And — believe it or not — you don't need their permission! As long as you only call in *highest good* energy, no harm or karmic violation can occur.

Even with the best intentions, you may not know what another person's highest good is. If you see someone suffering, you might naturally want to relieve their pain. But what if that isn't always the best choice?

Imagine this:

What if someone is in a challenging situation *that was carefully arranged by their higher self*? And what if that challenge, once mastered *through their own efforts*, gives them an essential breakthrough?

What if, by taking that challenge away — by helping too much, or solving it for them — *you unintentionally sabotage the main reason they incarnated?*

What if this is supposed to be their last human lifetime? At long last, they're ready to break the wheel of incarnation. They're about to ascend to the next level of their soul evolution!

But now, they have to do another round of human incarnation — because you interfered.

Do you know what happens if you help a newborn butterfly break free from its chrysalis? Or if you don't let a hatching chick peck out of its egg by itself?

If you help them, the newborn butterfly or chick usually doesn't survive. If they're going to live, they have to break out on their own. In the same way, *sometimes a suffering human needs to develop the strength to solve a major challenge on their own.*

I'm certainly not telling you to be cold or uncaring. You would ideally exercise such wise restraint, *when it's appropriate,* with deep compassion and unconditional love.

With Great Power Comes Great Responsibility

Why am I making such a big deal about this? Because when you flow energy, you're practicing genuine magic. You're consciously harnessing spiritual power. And, as every Spider-Man fan knows, "With great power comes great responsibility."

With power also comes potential danger. You could say, "I now flow energy to *force* this specific thing to happen." The Law of Free Will allows this. But can you be absolutely certain that what you're calling forth serves the highest good of all?

You certainly don't want to unintentionally cause harm when you're only trying to help. And you definitely don't want to burden yourself with bad karma by taking unwise action.

So, I recommend you play it safe. *Only ask for highest good energy to flow.* If the highest good of that being is to receive no energy through you, then nothing will happen.

The Karma-Free Safety Clause

When I do shamanic healing work, people routinely ask me for specific outcomes. A client might say, "I want my right shoulder to be completely healed and function perfectly."

I might invoke, "Divine allies, please completely heal this person's right shoulder and restore it to perfect functionality... *to the greatest extent that serves highest good, this or something better, thank you.*"

Those last fourteen words — *"to the greatest extent that serves highest good, this or something better, thank you"* — are critically important. I call them the *Karma-Free Safety Clause*.

As I said earlier, the safest course of action is to simply ask for highest good energy and leave it at that. But if you feel called to invoke a specific outcome, the Karma-Free Safety Clause — as the name implies — puts you on karmically safe ground.

Flowing Energy to "Adversarial Allies"

At first, get comfortable flowing energy to people you like or love. Then, when you're ready, you can flow highest good energy to people who trigger you. But be aware that this can catalyze unhealed emotional wounds that this person stirs up in you.

This can feel challenging while it's happening. But you can also end up with a spontaneous bonus healing! If you still feel discomfort after the energy flow wraps up, you can do a Healing Invocation for yourself to help clear it.

The catalyst such people bring to your life can speed up your personal evolution. As Michael Newton describes in his wonderful book *Journey of Souls*, you and a person who brings you a challenge may have agreed to this arrangement before you incarnated. Your souls might have agreed that they would make your life difficult in specific ways to help you accelerate your soul growth.

So, I no longer call anyone an "enemy." I prefer the term "adversarial ally."

Advanced Experiences

When doing the Hollow Reed Invocation, it's common to

feel energy flowing through your body. As you become more sensitive, you may also feel what the energy is doing at its destination. You could even become one with the destination so that you experience *blending* instead of flow. This can increase the invocation's effectiveness.

You can also have energy flow into the past or future, or into different dimensions and universes.

These advanced Hollow Reed experiences might seem impossible until you reach a certain level of awakening. Then, they're just business as usual.

Speaking of awakening, you'll probably notice a stronger desire to help others as you awaken more deeply. This is a natural byproduct of your progress on the path of love and light.

Free from the Safety Clause?

Can you dispense with the Karma-Free Safety Clause if your ego and higher self are completely and permanently blended, and all your actions are divinely initiated?

This is possible (and magnificent!), but be very careful. The deeper you go into awakening, the subtler the pitfalls become.

A person can believe they're more awakened than they really are. Even if you are that profoundly awakened, using the Karma-Free Safety Clause will cause no harm. Invoking specific outcomes for others without it, if your actions aren't as divinely initiated as you think, could have unfortunate karmic consequences for you and your recipient(s).

The Power of Group Work

Flowing highest good energy to others is certainly helpful when you do it on your own. But its power is vastly multiplied when done in a group!

According to the extraordinary Law of One channeled information (free online at LawOfOne.info), every extra person who participates in a spiritual process *doubles* its power.

You might think that ten people working together would create ten times the power. But apparently, it works more like this: 1, 2, 4, 8, 16, 32, 64, 128, 256, 512, etc. Ten people working together create over *five hundred* times as much spiritual power as one person working alone. The more the merrier!

Obviously, joining others in spiritual service can be much more effective than doing it on your own. There are many groups doing this sort of thing in person and online.

In fact, you're welcome to join my online group events! As of this writing, I do a free public Zoom call on the first Monday of each month at 8:00 p.m. US Eastern Time. It's called "New Earth Support Team."

We first create a sacred container and invoke embodied awakening. Then we let our divine allies of love and light know we've come to serve the great global awakening. They take it from there! Our spiritual service is routinely rewarded with personal healing, spiritual upgrades, and profound bliss.

I also offer another free group call, which offers you a direct experience of healing and/or awakening, during the second half of each month. You're always welcome to join us.

These calls are associated with my "Awakening Plus" online membership for spiritual support. To see the current schedule and Zoom info, go to AstroShaman.com. Scroll down the home page to my blog section. There, you'll always find a post for the current month's Awakening Plus events.

I hope to see you at one of these events!

Bare-Bones Instructions for the Hollow Reed Invocation

Note how your body and subtle energy feel.

Decide where you want highest good energy to flow. It can be to one or more people, or one or more situations.

Say, **"Spirit that I am, please flow the energy through me to serve [name of the person(s) or situation(s)]'s highest good."**

After you say the words, let them go and passively feel energy or breath.

Don't deliberately visualize anything.

Don't use any effort to flow energy.

You don't have to use your hands.

Just be a passive pipeline. "I conduit!"

You may notice subtle energy flowing into your crown chakra and out the front of your body on its way to your recipient(s). If you feel this, let it flow on its own. Otherwise, rest in passive breath awareness.

You don't have to worry about the color of the energy, what spiritual plane(s) it's coming from, or which spiritual allies are helping. Your higher self has all this covered.

You'll probably feel significantly *better* after the energy flow.

You don't have to know the recipient's highest good. And you don't need their permission. As long as you only call in *highest good* energy, no harm or karmic violation can occur.

If you choose to invoke a specific outcome, be sure to use the Karma-Free Safety Clause: *"To the greatest extent that serves highest good, this or something better, thank you."*

You've learned a lot about invocations so far. But I'm especially excited about the next chapter, where you'll learn how to call in any energy you want!

CHAPTER SEVEN: INVOCATION CONSTRUCTION KIT

So far, you've learned how to invoke your own embodied awakening and healing. You've also learned how to invoke highest good healing for others.

But the sky's the limit for invocations. They're endlessly versatile!

You can create new invocations anytime. Just plug the right words into a simple formula. Ask for whatever shift of energy or consciousness you want.

Anjuli is a big fan of this approach:

> After eight years of working with the invocations, I've gotten more creative and playful with them. This is such a great addition to the standard invocations I've come to love over the years.

— Anjuli

Once again, step-by-step instructions follow, supplemented with helpful information. The bare-bones instructions are at the end of this chapter.

The "Invocation Construction Kit" Formula

First, I'll give you the formula. Then I'll tell you more about how it works.

Here's the formula:

1. Start with the word "Maximum."

2. Describe the energy shift you want. Use simple, clear language.

3. Add "to the greatest extent that serves highest good, please."

4. Close with "this or something better, thank you."

Let's break this down in detail.

Fill In the Blank

Describe the energy shift you want. Use simple, clear language.

Here are some examples:

Saturate me with bliss.

Make me one with my higher self.

Integrate my light body and physical body.

Here's one from Donna:

> I use some variations of my own, spontaneously, as the need arises. *"Maximum Divine integration of my whole being that serves highest good, please"* is one that really resonates with me.
>
> — Donna M.

Keep it simple. Use the smallest number of words that express your meaning. How would Ernest Hemingway say it?

"Maximum [fill in the blank]," followed by *"to the greatest extent that serves highest good, please."*

This says to Spirit, "Give me as much as I can handle — but don't overdo it!"

I've facilitated thousands of IDA Invocations. But, as far as I know, no one has ever been overwhelmed. This language keeps you safe!

What if you ask for something inappropriate, and the greatest amount that would serve highest good is zero? In that case, nothing will happen.

The Rest of the Words

Close with: "this or something better, thank you."

"This or something better" lets Spirit bless you with something even *more* wonderful! And it's just good manners to say, *"thank you."* Plus, gratitude increases abundance!

For the sake of efficiency, we can reduce this to the following shortcut:

"Maximum [fill in the blank] that serves highest good, please."

Joel makes this a regular part of his day:

> Benjamin's invocations have really helped push me back into Presence. They are so easy and powerful, and I can use them throughout the day whenever I need a charge-up from Spirit.
>
> For example, I will say either out loud or to myself, *"Maximum surrender that serves highest good, please."* Then I'll feel my body until I notice the energy shift.
>
> I use different words throughout the day, depending on what I need, such as *"maximum presence"* or *"maximum vitality."* They have a way of realigning me with Spirit whenever I need it.
>
> — Joel Derrick

Roll Your Own!

Ready to "roll your own"? You're welcome to play with any or all of the following invocations.

Most of these create states of consciousness you might experience with the previous IDA Invocations. But if you take a shine to any of them, use them as often as you like!

Spiritual Awakening Invocation

"Spirit that I am, please grant me the maximum **spiritual**

awakening that serves highest good, this or something better, thank you."

Peace of Mind Invocation

"Spirit, please **lift me beyond the mental realm, to the level of intuitive clarity,** to the greatest extent that serves highest good, this or something better, thank you."

This invocation can merge your human awareness with your intuitive wisdom. This helps you simply *know* what to do, with no need for logic. This invocation can eliminate mental chatter and let you enjoy complete peace of mind.

Light Body Awareness Invocation

"Spirit that I am, please grant me the maximum **awareness of my light body** that serves highest good, this or something better, thank you."

Bliss Invocation

"Spirit that I am, please saturate me with the maximum **bliss** that serves highest good, this or something better, thank you."

Soak in bliss often! It feels great and automatically promotes healing. With your higher self saturating every cell of your human body, you receive constant healing in the background.

Light Body Expansion Invocation

"Spirit that I am, please **expand my light body to the hugest size** that serves highest good, this or something better, thank you."

You're actually the entire universe and all the dimensions of consciousness. You contain endless divine magnificence. There's no limit to how much of it you can ultimately become aware of. Think big!

Mark's Custom Invocations

Here are custom invocation ideas from Mark:

> I live in the UK and have been using Benjamin's invocations on a daily basis for over ten years. They've really helped me overcome my anxiety and lack of self-confidence. They also help me sleep at night when I get insomnia.
>
> As Benjamin suggests, I've created my own custom invocations using his template. The most helpful is, *"Spirit that I am, please give me guidance in this life that serves highest good, this or something better, thank you."* This one has really helped me make the right decisions over the last ten years, and has made my life easier and more enjoyable.
>
> — Mark Okrasa

Zachary Adama customizes the start of his IDA Invocations. Instead of "Spirit that I am," he starts with *"By my Great I Am Presence"* or *"By the God Within."* His divine aspect responds enthusiastically to these words!

How to Transform Ego-Based Techniques into Invocations

I'm not very good at visualization. I'm better at feeling than seeing in the inner worlds. I receive images as needed in my shamanic work, but that's about as far as it goes.

So, I was struggling one day when attending a live online

process. During a guided visualization, I wasn't seeing anything clearly in my mind's eye.

Then a possibility occurred to me. Could I *invoke* the visuals I needed? Would my higher self display them to me in real-time?

I crafted a custom invocation: *"Spirit that I am, please flow the images to me that I need to do this process effectively."*

It worked! Each time the facilitator asked us to imagine a mental picture, it appeared fully formed in my mind. My higher self created the images for me. As usual, it was happy to do for my ego what it couldn't do for itself.

I invite you to apply this idea to your current ego-directed spiritual practices. Are you doing something that requires visualization? Concentration? Or anything else that your higher self might be happy to do for you?

Surprising the Reiki Masters

I remember two different sessions I did for advanced Reiki Masters. As an experiment, I first had them flow healing Reiki energy to me as they usually did.

Then I had them flow highest good healing energy to me, using the Hollow Reed Invocation. They did this passively, without visualizing Reiki symbols as they normally would.

In both cases, they were amazed to feel significantly *more* healing power with the Hollow Reed Invocation. As the recipient, I also felt this amplified potency.

This idea has endless possibilities. **Why not invoke what you want — and passively receive a superior result — through the grace of your higher self?**

The next two sections don't entirely fit this chapter's "Invocation Construction Kit" theme, but at least they end with two custom invocations. So, this seems as good a spot as any for them!

A Prayer/Meditation Hybrid

The IDA Invocations merge prayer and meditation. This brings you the benefits of both approaches in a single system.

Prayer asks a higher power to give you something you want. Meditation is often practiced passively, as simply "being with what is."

Prayer gets the ball rolling by sharing your desire with a divine being who can help you. Meditation adds a crucial element lacking in many prayer practices: holding passive attention on your experience. This gives the divine a chance to give you what you asked for! In the IDA Invocations, prayer's *yang* partners perfectly with meditation's *yin*.

(Prayer and meditation can encompass much more than I include in these basic definitions. My goal here is to make a basic point, not address every possible prayer and meditation variation.)

As you know from my story in Chapter One, I didn't create the IDA Invocations by deliberately merging prayer and meditation. Ayahuasca simply downloaded them into my brain! My hope is that you might understand the IDA Invocations more deeply if I relate them to familiar spiritual techniques.

How the IDA Invocations Relate to Affirmations and the Law of Attraction

As long as we're comparing the IDA Invocations with other methods, let's consider affirmations and the Law of Attraction.

Affirmations proclaim that something is true. They don't require belief in a helpful divine being. A person doing an affirmation might simply believe in the power of thought to shift their experience. Or they might imagine the universe responding through vibrational resonance.

In my experience, the IDA Invocations shift reality faster and more effectively than the affirmation systems I'm aware of. This is because you've recruited your higher self to help you. In the numerous areas where your higher self can assist you, this potent divine ally is vastly more effective than your human self acting alone.

Law of Attraction work typically has a different focus than the IDA Invocations. The Law of Attraction usually focuses on *physical* manifestation, while the IDA Invocations specialize in *energetic* shifts. So, each technique works mostly within its own domain.

But these two techniques can play well together. For example, a Law of Attraction manifestation might be hindered by an unhealed trauma within you. If so, you can use the Healing Invocation to clear that emotional wound.

You're welcome to use these two custom invocations to empower your Law of Attraction work:

> For clearing: **"Spirit that I am, please clear or transmute any energies blocking what I'm calling in so that my desired outcome manifests to the greatest extent, and at the fastest rate, that serves highest good."**
>
> For energizing: **"Spirit that I am, please saturate me**

with those energies that will help my desired outcome manifest to the greatest extent, and at the fastest rate, that serves highest good."

Bare-Bones Instructions for the Invocation Construction Kit:

1. Start with the word "Maximum."

2. Describe the energy shift you want. Use simple, clear language.

3. Add "to the greatest extent that serves highest good, please."

4. Close with "this or something better, thank you."

Or use this shortcut: **"Maximum [fill in the blank] that serves highest good, please."**

We've spent a lot of time covering the details of the Instant Divine Assistance Invocations. In the next chapter, you'll learn why it's so important to do them consistently!

CHAPTER EIGHT: CONSISTENCY AND AMNESIA

Earlier in this book, I suggested that you do the Embodied Awakening Invocation every day. There's a critically important reason to do this.

Awakening Lost

In the years I've been sharing the Instant Divine Assistance Invocations, I've repeatedly witnessed a sad situation.

I'll be talking with a returning client. It could be weeks, months, or even years after our previous session. I'll ask them how their life is going. All too often, they're still stuck in the same challenging situations.

I'll say, "You learned the Embodied Awakening Invocation the last time we worked together. Did you keep doing it?" And they'll say something like, "Oh, I did it for a few days, but then I forgot about it. I got distracted. Life got in the way."

While they were doing it, they say, they felt great! They were experiencing the harmony, flow, ease, and grace of embodied awakening. There was way less mental chatter and challenging emotion. And they were feeling much more peaceful.

But then they stopped doing it… and slipped back into amnesia.

Their equanimity disappeared. Mental chatter and challenging emotions returned. Peacefulness gave way to suffering.

Avoiding Spiritual Amnesia

I don't want this to happen to you. Don't slip back into spiritual unconsciousness! Whatever practice works best to keep you awakened, whether it's mine or someone else's, I urge you to be consistent with it.

There's a major danger if you don't. *You could lose your awakening.* Slowly and subtly, without even realizing it, you could slip back into amnesia.

Before you know it, you'll be lost in delusion. You'll experience yourself as separate from everything else. And with that tragic misperception comes endless suffering and unhappiness.

Don't let yourself sink back into the misery most people stew in. You deserve better! That's why I strongly recommend that you *never take a day off from your invocation practice.*

Every morning, as soon as possible, say, **"Maximum embodied awakening that serves highest good, please."** Give your higher self a few seconds to merge with you. Let it saturate you with its peacefulness and euphoria. Witness all the mental chatter and challenging emotions falling away. Feel this beautiful state maintain itself effortlessly.

At that point, you're done. Move on with your day.

Will You Invest 10 Minutes to Stay Awakened All Day?

As I mentioned earlier, many clients tell me that this invocation gets them into embodied awakening in just five or ten seconds.

How much time do they usually spend refreshing it? Just five or ten minutes per day.

Think about that. *They invest just five or ten minutes*, a few seconds at a time, to do this simple, practically effortless invocation. In return, *they get to spend their entire day in a magnificent, awakened state*. Isn't that a great return on investment?

But what if they skip a day? And then another? And, before they know it, a few more days after that?

It would be so much easier if it was like a comic-book movie. The villain dominates the screen, roars their challenge, and faces the hero in a dramatic face-to-face confrontation.

If only it was that obvious. Instead, the darkness subtly slips in around the edges. You get more and more covered over — *and don't even know it's happening.*

Eventually, you're completely encased. The light of your divine awareness has shrunk from a bonfire to a candle flame.

You've sunk back into amnesia. You're once again locked into an endless cycle of suffering.

I've had so many people tell me how profoundly these

invocations have changed their lives. They say *they've never found any other system that requires so little time and effort... yet maintains and deepens embodied awakening so reliably*.

If you're going to use the IDA Invocations, I implore you: be persistent. *Don't skip a day — ever.* Rarely will so little effort reward you so richly!

Plus, *persistent daily practice will amplify your euphoria*. You're more likely to jump to new levels of awakening more quickly and consistently. Your new normal can become an ecstatic flow state... which even the world's finest poet could never describe.

How Can You *Not* Have Time to Save Hours a Day?

Some morning, a part of you will say, "I don't have time to do the Embodied Awakening Invocation right now. Maybe later."

Has this rebellious part forgotten that it might only take *a few seconds* to rekindle your embodied awakening? **Maybe less time than it took to read this two-sentence paragraph?**

Let's get real. Does a daily invocation practice cost you time, or save it?

You spend a lot of time making decisions each day. How much? I was astonished to learn that, according to many sources, *adults make about 35,000 "remotely conscious" decisions each day*. That isn't a typo: *thirty-five thousand*. For the average person, just deciding what food to put in their mouths eats up 227 daily decisions!

Granted, many of these are split-second decisions you instantly forget. But if you start paying attention, you'll see that you're making hundreds of *fully* conscious decisions each day. Some people make thousands of daily decisions!

What about in the business world? According to a 2018 McKinsey Global Survey (https://www.mckinsey.com/business-functions/people-and-organizational-performance/our-insights/decision-making-in-the-age-of-urgency), "Just over half of respondents report spending more than 30 percent of their working time on decision-making, and more than one-quarter spend a majority of their time making decisions ... On average, 61 percent say most of their decision-making time is used ineffectively. Among C-levels [top executives], 57 percent say the same."

It seems that people spend a lot of time making decisions... and they're not doing it efficiently.

But what if your intuition is driving, and you know what to do *immediately*? You might be able to save hours a day. *You can skip most of that logical decision-making... because your intuition already has the answer!*

This one's a total no-brainer. Doing a daily invocation practice won't *cost* you five or ten minutes a day. Instead, you might be able to *save* hours each day. And *think how much **effort** you'll save by not having to make all those decisions!*

So, you can absolutely justify taking time to do the Embodied Awakening Invocation every morning... and to refresh it as needed during the day. Even if the *only* benefit was all that time you save, you'd still come out ahead!

The World's Best Beauty Treatment

Here's one more incentive. An awakened state is the world's best beauty treatment!

The most dramatic example I ever saw was a woman in her seventies. She went to India and had a major spiritual awakening. When she came back, she looked like she was forty! I couldn't believe how young and radiant she looked.

Your spiritual makeover may not be this dramatic, but you should be able to easily see it for yourself. Just take selfies before and after you get into embodied awakening.

You'll see the difference. There's a sparkle in the eyes. The skin looks younger. Wrinkles can become less prominent or even disappear. There's something magical about an awakened person that radiates beauty on all levels — including *physical* beauty.

Donna noticed this:

> Benjamin's invocations have made a big difference for me. When I look in the mirror, I see less strain in my eyes, face, and neck. I feel like there's more of Me inside. It's beginning to feel natural to connect with my heart.
>
> — Donna M.

If you can't make yourself do the Embodied Awakening Invocation for any other reason, do it for the sake of vanity!

How to Stay Consistent

Earlier in this chapter, you learned about the dangers of spiritual amnesia. I made a big deal about being consistent with the Embodied Awakening Invocation. I emphasized how critically important it is to do it every day without fail.

It's easy to have good intentions. But even if you decide to maintain a daily invocation practice, how can you make sure you actually *do* it every day?

That's the challenge Laura faced:

> I'm on a journey in search of a better quality of life. I used to believe I'd be happy if I got to travel, or if my husband would stop ruining things, or if I made more money. I had experienced bliss here and there, but contentment was fleeting.
>
> At first, I tried to do the Embodied Awakening Invocation daily but kept forgetting. I wrote it down and stuck the paper in my wallet as a reminder. But I wouldn't always see it at the right time.
>
> Then I put the paper in my cosmetics drawer. As it turned out, this was a good strategy! Every morning, I'd go into the bathroom and pull out my makeup drawer. Then I'd see the paper. This would remind me to do the invocation.
>
> I noticed that when I didn't do this, things started getting fuzzy later in the day. Once I didn't need to read it on the paper anymore, I combined it with the Shavasana resting period of my morning yoga practice.
>
> I repeat the invocation as needed throughout the day to make sure my heart is open. This has become a habit I hope to always continue.
>
> As a result of Benjamin's invocation, my life has vastly improved. Nothing has changed, mind you. But all of a sudden I'm so happy with where I am, who I'm with, what I do for a living, and pretty much everything.
>
> My husband is happier too, and he doesn't do the

invocation yet. So far, I've been keeping it to myself. But he's happier because I'm happier.

I say the invocation daily to be my best self in times of stress, and to remain connected to Source.

— Laura R. Peterson

Laura describes a wonderful consistency strategy: having a regular daily event that reminds her to do the Embodied Awakening Invocation. At first, it's seeing the instructions in her cosmetics drawer. Later, she integrates it into her yoga practice. (In his supremely helpful book *Atomic Habits*, James Clear calls linking one habit to another "habit stacking.")

I do something similar. I follow a routine when I do my morning spiritual practice. The Embodied Awakening Invocation is one of the first things I do. And I routinely call in the Healing Invocation about halfway through.

Even after my abiding awakening in 2012, there was one period when I started to slip back down into the darkness. I wasn't doing a consistent spiritual practice, and my neglect was catching up with me.

I remember how this creeping amnesia made me feel more and more miserable, until I was finally able to rekindle and stabilize my awakening again. A consistent spiritual practice is as important for me as for anybody!

Phone Reminders

You might find electronic reminders helpful. You could set a recurring phone alarm every morning, to remind you to do the Embodied Awakening Invocation.

In addition, to guard against spiritual amnesia, you could set a few more daily alarms. These alarms could say something cute like, "Got light body?" They'd remind you to check in with yourself — are you still in embodied awakening? — and refresh it if you aren't.

Accountability Partner

You could also work with an accountability partner. They could check in with you each morning to ask if you've done your Embodied Awakening Invocation yet. If they're also doing it, you could do the same for them.

You and your accountability partner (or, if you prefer, "check-in buddy" or "accountabilibuddy") can touch base as often as you wish. You two will soon find your sweet spot: frequently enough to stay on track, but not so often that it's annoying.

By the way, having an accountability partner is *not* a sign of weakness or inadequacy. Many of the world's highest achievers pair up with one.

And for good reason. Because someone's holding them accountable, they dramatically increase the likelihood of achieving their goals!

Research supports this. According to an entrepreneur.com post ((https://www.entrepreneur.com/article/310062), the Association for Talent Development [the world's largest professional association for learning and talent development professionals] found that "people are 65 percent likely to meet a goal after committing to another person. *Their chances of success increase to **95 percent** when they build in ongoing meetings with their partners to check in on their progress.*" (Italics and bolding added.

Once you experience the benefits of the Instant Divine Assistance Invocations, you might feel inspired to share them with others. You may find it much easier to stay on track if a friend or loved one is doing them with you as your accountability partner.

It's ideal if your accountability partner reads this book, but that's not absolutely necessary. Just point them to **"Instant Divine Assistance: Your Free Guide to Fast and Easy Awakening and Healing"** at **astroshaman.com/invocations**. There they'll learn the essentials of the IDA Invocations.

The Difficulty of Starting and Maintaining a New Habit

Here's a sobering truth. *If you don't begin a new habit immediately, chances are you never will.*

How many times have you been genuinely excited about doing something? You honestly mean to get started… and then a day goes by, and a week, and a month… but you never actually get around to it. For most people, this is a sadly familiar pattern.

And what if you're one of the few who actually do get started? How often do you actually *lock in* a new habit? Have you ever been like one of those people who enthusiastically join a health club at the start of January, but stop working out by the beginning of February?

You may have heard that it takes 21 days to establish a new habit. But recent research tells a different story. It can take 18 to 254 days to lock in a new habit. The average time is 66 days.

Most people simply can't stick it out that long… at least, not without help! So, here's a simple support system to help you maintain embodied awakening.

Free Invocation Reminder Emails

Most people find it easiest to establish a new habit with baby steps, then build up gradually. With this in mind, I've created a series of invocation reminders.

These automated reminders give you email support, for as long as you choose, to help you make embodied awakened your daily reality. And they're free!

The emails will be brief. You can easily stop or start these messages, or switch between the options, whenever you wish. And most feature two-line poems with a variety of inspiring messages.

You have four options to choose from:

> Four Daily Reminders, sent at 8 a.m., 12 p.m., 4 p.m., and 8 p.m.
>
> Four Daily Reminders, sent at 6 a.m., 10 a.m., 2 p.m., and 6 p.m.
>
> Two Daily Reminders, sent at 8 a.m. and 4 p.m.
>
> Two Daily Reminders, sent at 6 a.m. and 2 p.m.

This information was correct upon publication. The current program details and sign-up form are online.

Speaking of which, **why not sign up for your free email reminders now? Just visit InstantDivineAssistance.com.**

I also offer more free support to help you get the greatest benefit from the IDA Invocations. You'll learn about it in Chapter Eleven.

Never Miss Twice

What if you commit to doing the IDA Invocations every single day... and *still* miss a day? Then remember another pearl of wisdom from *Atomic Habits*: "Never miss twice!"

Reawakening Strategies

What if, despite your best efforts, you *do* slip into amnesia... and the Embodied Awakening Invocation doesn't rekindle your divine awareness?

Fortunately, there are three fallback strategies for this. I recommend trying them in this order.

1. On your own, do the full Embodied Awakening Invocation Cycle described in Chapter Nine.

2. If that doesn't work, use the recording of the Embodied Awakening Invocation Cycle at **InstantDivineAssistance.com.** My voice will guide you through the cycle step by step. Hopefully, this will get you realigned with your higher self.

3. If even that doesn't do it, get an awakened person to help you. [I do this for clients in my Shamanic Healing/IFS sessions (https://www.astroshaman.com/services/shamanic-healing/)].

This ends Part One. Congratulations! You've read eight chapters, and only have four more to go! You've now learned enough to do the Instant Divine Assistance Invocations effectively.

Let's move on to Part Two. It opens by introducing you to a deeper, richer experience of awakening… by doing the Embodied Awakening Invocation Cycle.

PART TWO: DIVING DEEPER

CHAPTER NINE: THE EMBODIED AWAKENING INVOCATION CYCLE

Let me introduce you to the four-step Embodied Awakening Invocation Cycle.

You've learned the eight-word shortcut for embodied awakening. But here comes the deluxe version!

Free Recording

To enjoy the deepest experience, go to InstantDivineAssistance.com for a free recording. I'll guide you through the entire Embodied Awakening Invocation Cycle!

The Four Invocations in This Cycle

There are four invocations in this cycle:

1. Your higher self saturates you with the maximum light and divine consciousness that serve highest good.

2. You merge with your higher self at its level, experiencing yourself as pure blissful energy.

3. Your higher self merges with you in your physical body.

4. You ask to consistently maintain the consciousness of your higher self from now on, to the greatest extent that serves highest good, with optimal physical functionality.

There's a richness and sweetness to this longer process you don't get with the shortcut. Most notably — and blissfully! — this cycle gives you a chance to *merge with your higher self in the spiritual realm*. (The shortcut, optimized for speed and efficiency, skips this step.)

Also, the final invocation in this cycle asks to *maintain the maximum divine awareness that you can hold from now on, with optimal physical functionality*. With this invocation, people often experience tingling and upgrades in their brains.

These tingling and upgrade experiences don't happen as often with the shortcut. Some people also experience a deeper level of awakening during this fourth invocation.

Obviously, this process is more involved than the shortcut. If it seems too complicated, feel free to skip it. Everything else you learn in this book will still work just fine!

Should You Work with the Recording Now?

You might find it most helpful to read the rest of this chapter *after* you work with the recording. It contains all the instructions you need. The rest of this chapter is most helpful if you want to do this cycle on your own *without* the recording.

In the "Reawakening Strategies" section of Chapter Eight, you learned how to reawaken yourself if necessary. My first suggestion is to do the Embodied Awakening Invocation Cycle in this chapter on your own. If that's not enough, I suggest you work with the Embodied Awakening Invocation Cycle recording at InstantDivineAssistance.com.

You guessed it! Step-by-step instructions follow, supplemented with helpful information. If you just want the bare-bones instructions, they're at the end of the chapter as usual.

Let's Do the Embodied Awakening Invocation Cycle!

As a reminder, this process brings divine energy into your physical body. Then you awaken to the absolute peace of your higher self at its level. Finally, you integrate this exquisite peacefulness into your everyday life.

The First Invocation: Maximum Light and Divine Consciousness

Here's the first invocation:

"Spirit that I am, please saturate me with the maximum light and divine consciousness that serve highest good, this or something better, thank you."

After saying this first invocation, rest in passive awareness of subtle energy or breath, as previously described.

The Second Invocation: Merge Me with the Peacefulness of My Higher Self at Its Level

Once you start feeling peaceful, do the second invocation:

"**Spirit that I am, please merge me with the peacefulness of my higher self at its level, to the greatest extent that serves highest good, this or something better, thank you.**"

After saying this invocation, shift your awareness to feel peacefulness. Rest in simple awareness of whatever peacefulness you already feel.

Play the Minimum Effort Game (see Chapter Two), dropping your effort level to zero. Do you still feel the peacefulness? If not, add the *absolute minimum effort* needed to feel the peacefulness.

As this invocation takes effect, the peacefulness will grow stronger all by itself. Soon you'll start feeling light or floaty. Eventually, you'll feel like a cloud of energy or ball of light.

You'll experience yourself as pure energy, with no shape or form. You'll feel exquisitely peaceful. And you won't experience any mental chatter or challenging emotions.

Once you're having this experience, congratulations! You've awakened to your higher self.

Rest in your peaceful light body. At this level, there's nowhere to go and nothing to do. But it feels amazing!

Enlightening Questions to Ask while Merged

Once you've merged with your higher self, it can be enlightening to ponder the following questions:

> What feels more real: my peaceful light body or my physical body?
>
> What if my more fundamental identity is this peaceful ball of energy instead of my physical body?
>
> What if my physical body is like a rental car that I use for a few decades?
>
> What if my human part could enjoy the same exquisite peacefulness as my divine part? What if this soul-deep ecstasy, free of mental chatter and challenging emotion, could be my human self's "new normal"?

How wonderful would your life be then?

Review of Embodied Awakening Core Benefits

I've mentioned the core benefits of embodied awakening a lot. You might even have them memorized by now:

> You'll enjoy more harmony, flow, ease, and grace daily.
>
> Whatever you're responsible for, you'll do *more* responsibly — and more joyfully!
>
> Instead of having to figure everything out, you'll make more decisions intuitively, and…
>
> You'll enjoy more euphoria in everything you do.

People often say, "It doesn't get any better than this." But after you experience these ecstatic divine states, you'll have a new motto: "It *always* gets better than this!"

The Third Invocation: Embodied Awakening Invocation (Longer Version)

Now, do this invocation:

"Spirit that I am, please integrate my physical and spiritual bodies to the greatest extent that serves highest good, thank you."

Return to passively feeling energy or breath. Use the minimum effort needed to maintain this awareness.

Once your physical and spiritual bodies have merged, it can be helpful to ask yourself the following questions. Be sure to feel deeply into each question before asking the next one.

Questions to Gain Deep Awareness of Embodied Awakening

Do I have full awareness of my physical body?

Do I have full awareness of my peaceful light body?

Can I feel both bodies at once?

Are my physical and spiritual bodies so integrated that it's hard to tell them apart?

Do I feel smooth electricity in my physical body? And is that electricity comfortable?

Am I free of mental chatter and challenging emotions?

Do I feel deeply peaceful?

> Is this new consciousness maintaining itself without effort?

As you already know, you're in embodied awakening once all the following are true: deep peacefulness, no mental chatter or challenging emotions, and the state maintaining itself. Even if you're partway there, it's still a wonderful step forward!

Once you've achieved embodied awakening, luxuriate in this exquisite consciousness for a moment or two. Then ask yourself:

"Which do I prefer? How I feel now, or how I usually feel every day?"

The Fourth Invocation: Strong, Consistent, and Ever-Deepening Embodied Awakening

If you prefer how embodied awakening feels, would you like this to become your new normal? *Remember that you can fulfill all your responsibilities **more** responsibly and joyfully in this state.*

If you said yes — as most everyone does — then say the fourth and final invocation in this cycle:

"Spirit that I am, please grant me the most strong, consistent, and ever-deepening embodied awakening that serves highest good, this or something better, thank you."

Rest in passive awareness of energy or breath, using minimum effort. You may feel a significant energy shift in your body. Unusual energetic phenomena may occur as your higher self upgrades you to hold embodied awakening more powerfully and consistently. You may feel this most strongly in your brain.

Just let this happen. Trust that your higher self knows what it's doing — because it does! Remain passive until the energy has stabilized.

Physically Active Embodied Awakening: Come Out Swinging!

Next, open your eyes and look around the physical space you're in. Is your embodied awakening holding steady, on its own, as you visually engage with the physical world?

It can be fun at this point to swing one of your arms in a wide arc. Do you feel your tingly energy arm moving in sync with your physical arm?

Once you feel that, it can be easier to feel the same tingly energy throughout your body. This is that "smooth electricity" mentioned earlier.

This completes the four-step invocation cycle. Now you can enjoy the profound benefits of embodied awakening in everything you do!

Bare-Bones Instructions for the Four-Step Embodied Awakening Invocation Cycle

> Say the first invocation: **"Spirit that I am, please saturate me with the maximum light and divine consciousness that serve highest good, this or something better, thank you."**
>
> Once you start feeling peaceful, say the second invocation: **"Spirit that I am, please merge me with the peacefulness of my higher self at its level, to the greatest extent that serves highest good, this or something better, thank**

you."

After saying this invocation, shift your awareness to feel peacefulness.

Play the Minimum Effort Game until you experience yourself as exquisitely peaceful energy beyond your physical body. Bask here as long as you like.

When you're ready, say: **"Spirit that I am, please integrate my physical and spiritual bodies to the greatest extent that serves highest good, this or something better, thank you."**

Return to passively feeling energy or breath. Use the minimum effort needed to maintain this awareness until you're in embodied awakening.

If you prefer the way you feel now to your usual consciousness, say: **"Spirit that I am, please grant me the most strong, consistent, and ever-deepening embodied awakening that serves highest good, this or something better, thank you."**

Relax and let the divine energy run its course. When it's done, see if your embodied awakening holds steady with your eyes open.

Optional: as you swing an arm, do you feel your tingly energy arm moving in sync with your physical arm? Can you feel tingly energy throughout your body?

This completes the four-step invocation cycle. Now you can enjoy the profound benefits of embodied awakening in everything you do!

You've now learned both basic and advanced ways to use the IDA Invocations. Next, you'll learn how to use them in specific life situations!

CHAPTER TEN: INVOCATIONS FOR SPECIFIC CHALLENGES

You've learned how to use the Instant Divine Assistance Invocations to help with your awakening, healing, service to others, and more. But these invocations can help with just about anything!

In this chapter, you'll learn how the IDA Invocations can help you with letting go, life direction, relationships, sleep, alertness, and work. You'll learn invocations to help you with specific psychological challenges, any 12-Step program you're doing, and your seven chakras. And you'll get to enjoy four in-depth healing stories!

Letting Go

Beverly's story weaves together several themes, including how invocations helped her learn to let go:

When I faced one of the biggest challenges of my life, I was working *more* than full-time. I was working as a cosmetologist, coaching gymnastics, raising two daughters, and running a household. My parents had moved in next door, and I was helping them. And I was dealing with my siblings' life issues — which my parents enabled! Even though I was doing so much, I barely let my partner help me.

Then one day I had a freak fall getting out of a truck. I broke my back.

In that moment, everything changed. I was unable to work. Things boiled over with my parents. They moved out of the house next door and completely disowned me. Then my oldest daughter moved out of the house — at the same time that my youngest was graduating and getting ready to leave for college!

I had no choice but to finally allow help from my partner. I was now at one of the lowest points of my life. I felt so alone.

Fortunately, I found Benjamin's in-person meditation group. It was meeting once a week in Asheville.

The way he conducted his meditations, inviting helpful spirits from many different paths and traditions, made me feel right at home. I could feel all the spirits coming in. This brought me a sense of peace I couldn't find otherwise.

Then Benjamin added his invocations at the beginning of the meditation. A part of myself moved out of the way, letting a more peaceful part step in.

This allowed me to finally feel a complete 'rest' of my

soul. At long last, I didn't feel all the hurt, shame, blame, frustration, and anger that had been so hard to deal with.

I'd been pummeled by these negative feelings every day. I had lost everything I thought I was. I didn't know anything about me at all.

At this desperate moment, Benjamin's invocations helped me find balance and peace. They helped me start relaxing my fanatical level of control, which was making my life so much harder than it needed to be.

I started feeling amazing things I'd never experienced before. I started to understand how to feel and work with energy outside of me. I started to let things flow through naturally. I stopped needing to control everything in every moment!

To this day, I still sometimes find myself thinking that I know best, or that things have to be a certain way. But, thanks to Benjamin's invocations, now I know that I can always invite my higher self in and just... let... go.

This has really helped me in my journey toward deeper understanding, self-growth, and peace. I now feel connected to my spirit team at all times.

I am beyond grateful for all this! I feel so blessed that — while I'm still figuring out who I am — I can always use Benjamin's invocations to help ground me and find my inner calmness.

— Beverly Rickard

Letting go more easily happened naturally for Beverly, as a wonderful side effect of her invocation work. This might happen for you too. Or you could call it in with this custom invocation:

*"Maximum **ease of letting go**, to the greatest extent that serves highest good, this or something better, thank you."*

Life Direction

The IDA Invocations helped Hannah reestablish her life direction after a disorienting move. As with Beverly, this clarity was a side effect that came without her asking:

> I moved to Asheville from New Orleans after Hurricane Katrina. I fell in love with Asheville and Benjamin's group.
>
> In New Orleans, I had a strong identity. I had two businesses, both in the creative field. All of it was washed away by Katrina.
>
> In Asheville, I was floundering. Who was I here? What did I have to offer? What were my next steps?
>
> Stagnation was settling in on my spirituality, emotional health, and creativity. I felt lonely and didn't know what to do next.
>
> It helped me to attend Benjamin's live groups, pre-COVID. I was able to open my heart and mind as Benjamin invoked Pachamama [Mother Earth] and the energies of the four directions. We did healing work and I released my fears.
>
> In the course of the group work Benjamin gave the following invocation. I end my daily meditations with it:
>
> *"Spirit that I am, please saturate me with your healing, loving light. Please clear from me all energy that does not serve my highest good, this or something better, thank you."*
>
> In only a few weeks, I was able to let my "mind" go

and let this amazing invocation integrate with my energy field. My creative energies began to flow again. My lack of direction disappeared. New ideas and channels for creative expression appeared.

So many wonderful things have happened since my work with Benjamin's invocations! I have written two books and am working on a third. I've purchased a home. And I've developed many friendships and co-creative partnerships.

Invoking saturation of the healing love and light is so powerful. It burns away the obstacles that prevent me from moving forward, feeling connected, and creating a rewarding life. I am so grateful to Benjamin and his beautiful work!

— Hannah Desmond

As Hannah experienced, all sorts of wonderful things can spontaneously happen when you consistently use the Healing Invocation. Or, to specifically request your higher self's help in aligning with your true north, you could say:

*"Maximum **clarity of life direction**, to the greatest extent that serves highest good, this or something better, thank you."*

Relationships

RT used the Invocation Construction Kit to make a relationship healing invocation:

I routinely use Benjamin's invocations with any problem I'm having, including relationships. I'll say, *"Spirit, **please bring the maximum amount of healing to this relationship**. May this be so to the greatest extent that serves highest good, this or something better, thank you."*

— RT

The IDA Invocations support Anjuli's family relationships:

> My mom and sister also use the Embodied Awakening Invocation, and my boyfriend loves to use it. Sometimes we'll turn to one another and just say, "Oh, let's do the invocation! It'll calm the energy of the whole space." So, it's improving my relationships as well, and it's an absolute delight to use!
>
> — Anjuli

Can you imagine a wonderful world where people routinely use tools like the IDA Invocations to heal relationship friction?

Sleep

In Chapter Three, Anjuli said that the Healing Invocation had improved her sleep. And Mark Okrasa said that the invocations "help me sleep at night when I get insomnia."

RT has a custom invocation ready when he has trouble dozing off:

> I use an invocation for sleep problems, since I tend to wake up at 4:00 a.m. with my mind racing and ruminating. Let's face it, these are stressful times. Who knows what's going to happen next in this crazy world of ours!
>
> Before I learned Benjamin's invocations, I might have taken Ambien, Xanax, or Benadryl. But now I just say, "Spirit, please grant me **the maximum amount of your divine peace and rest**, right now. May this be so to the greatest extent that serves highest good, thank you."

This is a highly effective sedative. It brings me peace, and I fall back to sleep.

— RT

Alertness

Anjuli, Mark, and RT use invocations to help them sleep. But I recently had to craft a custom invocation to keep sleep away!

I was sitting in my office, working with a shamanic life-coaching client. Let's call him Paul. I hadn't gotten a full night's sleep for the prior three nights and was already drowsy when he arrived.

My alertness was also challenged by the fact that Paul has an *extremely* soothing baritone voice. If I were hiring someone to narrate bedtime stories, with the specific purpose of putting kids to sleep, he'd be the one. And he launched into a series of extended monologues that, from my semiconscious perspective, seemed to go on forever!

I could have stayed alert more easily with more opportunities to speak, but Paul's nonstop "worderfall" gave me no openings. This forced me into a passivity that increasingly shaded into unconsciousness....

Until, finally, unconsciousness won. The next thing I remembered was jerking awake in my chair, seeing Paul staring at me — and realizing I'd passed out. And he'd been talking about something really important!

Yes, I was embarrassed. Fortunately, I was able to use this predicament as a teaching opportunity.

"Okay," I said, "I guess there's no hiding the fact that I just fell asleep while you were talking. I'm so sorry. I've been short on sleep lately.

"Let's see if I can come up with an invocation that will help me stay alert, so I can give you the attention you deserve." Paul had already been crafting custom invocations, so he knew what I was talking about.

I started with a custom healing invocation. *"Spirit that I am,"* I said, *"**please clear the energy of fatigue and sleepiness from my field**, to the greatest extent that serves highest good, this or something better, thank you."*

I went passive and immediately felt heavy energy flush from my hands and feet. The flush only took a few seconds. I already felt more alert, but there was one more invocation to go.

"Spirit that I am," I said, *"**maximum alertness, focus, and conscious presence** that serves highest good, please."* As I once again relaxed into passivity, I felt energy pour into my crown chakra from above. I felt my body quickly saturate with the energies I'd requested. Once again, the entire process only took a few seconds.

The invocations were effective. For the rest of our session, I was effortlessly focused, present, and alert. It's amazing what your higher self can give you, if you just bother to invoke it and receive it!

Work

The IDA Invocations can also help you at work. RT shared this remarkable story:

> I was a law enforcement officer for thirty years, and am now retired.

Once I had to interview an extremely vicious incarcerated serial killer for two-and-a-half days. I happened to have had my yearly astrology consultation with Benjamin right before that. With this challenging encounter ahead of me, I had asked Benjamin for an invocation I could use to support me.

Talking to this serial killer was terrifying. But I used the Embodied Awakening Invocation before meeting with him, during breaks between our interviews, and any time I needed a boost.

I also invoked, *"Spirit that I am,* **please flow through me the maximum amount of your divine peace and love toward Bill.** (Not the serial killer's real name.) *May this be so to the greatest extent that serves highest good, thank you."*

And it worked! I gained some form of rapport with him. What Bill did was horrible. But over the course of two-and-a-half days, he admitted to nine more murders!

— RT

Anjuli's next story is less dramatic than RT's. But she describes how invocations can help in a more common work situation:

One thing that I love about the invocations is that they're so clean and clear and direct... and easily customized!

Here's a recent example. I had a presentation at work for a department that we've had difficult relationships with. And I could feel that in the beginning of the meeting.

So, under my breath, I did a variation of the invocations: *"Spirit that I am,* **please flow calming energy through me to help smooth this environment and help improve relations between the departments. Let me be that beacon of light."**

The meeting was almost instantaneously calmed! I just got to sit and breathe within it. And when I did my presentation, I really did feel that everybody got on board. It was exciting to see! And I got so much positive feedback afterward.

I love opening myself to the flow that the invocations allow, which makes them a fantastic tool at work. I can use them before an interview, or any time I'm working with other people. It's so great to flow that energy through, and also get that bounce!

— Anjuli

Sarah used the IDA Invocations to help her transition between jobs:

In January 2021 I quit a job which had stretched me to the max. It had totally burned me out with long hours and very demanding work. I was looking for a way to move past that terrible feeling of stress and burnout.

I took up running, which helped me get out of my head and back into my body. I also started saying the embodiment invocation while I ran. I slightly altered it to be, "**Maximum embodied awakening** *that serves highest good* **— with gratitude!**"

I added "with gratitude" to assume success and amplify the manifestation process. Plus, it's fun to say *"with gratitude"* as I do jazz hands!

Several times, I felt tingly in my hands after I entered the space of the invocation. I felt that I was radiating heat and light — even when I was running in temperatures near zero degrees!

Benjamin's invocation helped me accept that I needed to regain strength and heal. I felt more confident that things would work out.

I resumed a job hunt — but very discerningly. I only applied to companies that I truly respected and felt were healthy places to work.

A few weeks before my unemployment checks ended, a friend from my old job called. He offered me a part-time job at his new place of work. The wage was equal to my old salary — for half the hours!

The whole process of quitting, looking for work, and starting a new job was surprisingly seamless and easy. Being so burned out, I wasn't sure I could return to an office job. But I was able to heal, be present in my body, and discover a healthy solution. I've been very happy in my new role.

Using this invocation makes it easier for me to trust my divine guidance. I have a much better time of things when I trust than when I overthink. Plus, it just feels great. I'm so grateful to Benjamin for this beautiful channeling!

— Sarah

In our final career example, the IDA Invocations helped Amanda, a professional artist, improve her painting:

I'm an artist but hadn't been able to concentrate. However, after doing the invocations, I was able to focus on my art for longer periods. When I went to the beach, I was able to see new colors and details in the sunrise and the ocean and capture them on my canvases. My artistic vision became a lot more clear.

— Amanda Elwell

By the way, if you have a professional practice — especially one that helps people heal or awaken — you have my blessing and encouragement to use the IDA Invocations with your clients. The more people that are helped by these invocations, the better!

Animal Attraction

Do you love animals? If so, here's a story for you!

> I started doing Benjamin's invocations on the beach at sunrise. After a while, dogs and birds started coming around.
>
> Once, when I was sitting in lotus position with my eyes closed, a little dog came and sat in my lap. And it wouldn't leave!
>
> Her owner said, "How weird is that? My dog is usually scared of people. I've never seen her sit on a stranger's lap before!"
>
> Animals had never been attracted to me before, but now it was like they wouldn't stay away. Dogs would come and say hello, and their owners consistently said that their pets weren't usually friendly with people.
>
> — Amanda Elwell

As her divine light got brighter, Amanda found herself spontaneously attracting animals. As you consistently work with the IDA Invocations, don't be surprised if you start attracting all sorts of wonderful things into your life!

Invocations for Specific Psychological Challenges

I want this book to help you as much as possible. So, I researched the most common psychological challenges. Then I created the following variations to help you with any of these challenges you might be experiencing.

I've done over 10,000 client sessions as an astrologer, shamanic healer, and life coach. So when I found an authoritative website on common psychological challenges — the nonprofit Anxiety & Depression Association of America (ADAA) — what I read there was familiar from many of my clients' stories.

All statistics in the following section are from the ADAA site, accessed on May 19, 2022. But the site has lots more valuable information. Visit https://adaa.org/understanding-anxiety/facts-statistics to learn more about these disorders.

I've worked with many clients who suffer from the psychological challenges that the ADAA describes. And I've frequently seen these invocations fully or partially heal them.

I can't guarantee a particular outcome for you. But, as you learned earlier, invoking your divine power can result in miraculous cures — which could exceed what you thought was possible.

So, it's worth a shot! If an IDA Invocation completely clears a psychological challenge, you can put it behind you and enjoy a happier life. If an invocation gives you partial healing, you can include it in your therapeutic mix. If it's not effective, drop it and try something different.

Anxiety

According to the World Health Organization (WHO), one in thirteen globally suffers from anxiety. The WHO reports that anxiety disorders are the most common mental disorders worldwide.

Anxiety disorders are the most common mental illness in the US, affecting forty million adults in the United States ages eighteen and older (18.1 percent of the population) every year. Fortunately, anxiety disorders are highly treatable.

When working with specific challenges, it's good practice to invoke its positive opposite. What's the opposite of anxiety? Calmness. So, if you're feeling anxious, try this invocation:

*"Maximum **calmness** that serves highest good, this or something better, thank you."*

Hold passive awareness where you feel the anxiety most strongly. Then proceed with the standard Healing Invocation follow-up you learned in Chapter Three.

This could be helpful in many cases where anxiety arises, no matter what triggers it.

Generalized Anxiety Disorder (GAD)

Anxiety is a broad term that includes more specific disorders. One is Generalized Anxiety Disorder (GAD). GAD affects 6.8 million adults, or 3.1 percent of the US population.

GAD is characterized by persistent and excessive worry about many things. The *Maximum Calmness Invocation* could be a good place to start. Once again, that's:

*"Maximum **calmness** that serves highest good, this or something better, thank you."*

Given the intensely mental nature of GAD, you might also find the Thought-Focused Invocation in Chapter Five helpful. That's the one with the two-story thought house visualization.

Panic Disorder (PD)

Panic Disorder (PD) affects six million adults, or 2.7 percent of the US population. I also recommend the Maximum Calmness Invocation for this.

Social Anxiety Disorder (SAD)

Social Anxiety Disorder (SAD) affects fifteen million adults, or 6.8 percent of the US population. With this, try the following custom invocation: *"Maximum **calmness and confidence in social situations** that serve highest good, this or something better, thank you."*

Specific Phobias

Specific Phobias affect nineteen million adults, or 8.7 percent of the US population. Phobias are "seemingly excessive and unreasonable fears in the presence of or in anticipation of a specific object, place, or situation." Common phobias include the fear of vomiting, driving, flying, needles, and health challenges.

This invocation might prove helpful: *"Maximum **ease and comfort when dealing with [name of phobia]** that serves highest* *good, this or something better, thank you."*

Obsessive-Compulsive Disorder (OCD)

Obsessive-Compulsive Disorder (OCD) affects 2.2 million adults, or 1.0 percent of the US population. For this, try: *"Maximum **ease and flow in doing what I choose** that serves highest good, this or something better, thank you."*

Post-Traumatic Stress Disorder (PTSD)

Post-Traumatic Stress Disorder (PTSD) affects 7.7 million adults, or 3.5 percent of the US population. Rape is the most likely trigger of PTSD: 65 percent of men and 45.9 percent of women who are raped will develop this disorder. Childhood sexual abuse is a strong predictor of a lifetime likelihood of developing PTSD.

The Healing Invocation can help heal any kind of trauma. I've had many clients use it successfully with PTSD. As a reminder, the Healing Invocation is: *"Maximum healing that serves highest good, please."*

Use the standard Healing Invocation if trauma from PTSD arises spontaneously. To voluntarily focus on a specific trauma, use the second Healing Invocation variation in Chapter Three. It's in the section called, "How to Proactively Heal a Past Trauma."

Depression

Depression is the leading cause of disability worldwide. Major Depressive Disorder is the leading cause of disability in the US for ages 15 to 44.3. It affects more than 16.1 million American adults (about 6.7 percent).

To help heal depression, do the standard Healing Invocation, then hold attention where the feeling of depression is strongest in your body. Another approach is to call in its opposite: *"Maximum **hopefulness** that serves highest good, please."*

Other Types of Anxiety

If you experience anxiety triggered by something not mentioned already, you can create a custom invocation for it. You can identify its positive opposite and use the Custom Invocation formula: *"Maximum [fill in the blank] that serves highest good, please."* You can also use the standard Healing Invocation ("Maximum healing that serves highest good, please"), before and/or after the Custom Invocation, if needed.

Bipolar Disorder Put on Hold by an Invocation

I recently did a healing session with Charlene, a client with bipolar disorder. In the early part of our session, her thoughts bounced around like a pinball. She couldn't stay on the same subject for more than a few seconds before jumping to an unrelated topic. ("Racing thoughts" and "distractibility" are listed on the Mayo Clinic web page that describes the symptoms of bipolar disorder, at https://www.mayoclinic.org/diseases-conditions/bipolar-disorder/symptoms-causes/syc-20355955.)

I drew Charlene's attention to this every time it happened, but even her best efforts couldn't stop it.

Then I remembered that a person's higher self can accomplish things an ego can't do on its own. I led her through the Embodied Awakening Invocation.

The moment Charlene entered embodied awakening, the racing thoughts and distractibility stopped on a dime! It was as if a light switch had turned on. *For the rest of our session, which lasted over an hour more, her attention was effortlessly single-pointed and focused.* We both marveled at how quickly and easily she had transitioned from manic bipolar energy to the calm serenity of divine consciousness.

Charlene has big things she wants to accomplish. But a condition as serious and deeply rooted as her bipolar disorder probably won't be eliminated by a one-shot invocation. I encouraged her to be diligent with the Embodied Awakening Invocation, doing it first thing every morning and repeating it as needed throughout the day.

For years, Charlene's hopes and dreams have been thwarted. She hasn't been able to focus on anything long enough to manifest it. But if she can make embodied awakening her "new normal," by sticking with a rigorous daily invocation practice, her odds of success will improve dramatically!

Empowering Your 12-Step Program with the IDA Invocations

If you're doing a 12-Step program, the IDA Invocations could prove especially helpful in Steps 7 and 11.

Step 7 asks a 12-Step participant to practice humility. They're encouraged to ask a higher power to remove their shortcomings, then replace them with spiritual practices. Bill W.'s "Big Book" summarizes this step as: "Humbly asked Him to remove our shortcomings."

As part of Step 7, participants are encouraged to do prayer, meditation, or other spiritual practices. To support this step, Alcoholics Anonymous (AA) offers this prayer:

> "My Creator, I am now willing that you should have all of me, good and bad. I pray that you now remove from me every single defect of character which stands in the way of my usefulness to you and my fellows. Grant me strength as I go out from here to do your bidding."

This custom healing invocation is based on the second sentence of that prayer:

> **"Spirit that I am, remove from me every single defect of character which stands in the way of my usefulness to you and my fellows, to the greatest extent that serves highest good, this or something better, thank you."**

Many people say the Step 7 prayer above, then immediately move along to something else without pausing. They don't stay passive enough, or leave enough time, for their higher self to act on their request with its full healing power.

But you can maximize the healing power of this prayer.

Each "defect of character" corresponds to an energetic block somewhere in your body. All you have to do is treat this invocation as a "Next in Line!" Healing Invocation, as described in Chapter Five. In a nutshell, notice where the energy is working and hold passive awareness there. As always, your higher self knows best how to heal you!

The Embodied Awakening Invocation plays well with Step 11:

"Sought through prayer and meditation to improve our conscious contact with God as we understood Him, praying only for knowledge of His will for us and the power to carry that out."

The Embodied Awakening Invocation will improve your "conscious contact with God" at its easiest access point: your higher self. Your improved intuition will give you greater "knowledge of His will for us." And the deeper your embodied awakening becomes, the more easily divine energy will flow through you. This will give you "the power to carry that out."

In case you haven't already memorized it, the Embodied Awakening Invocation shortcut is:

"Maximum embodied awakening that serves highest good, please."

Invocations for the Seven Chakras

If you want to work directly with your chakras, you can use the Instant Divine Assistance Invocations to clear and energize them. The IDA Invocations don't *require* chakra work, but it can be helpful.

In this section, you'll learn invocations for the seven major energy centers in your physical body. If you want to do invocations for minor or out-of-body chakras, you can create them using the Invocation Construction Kit in Chapter Seven.

These suggested invocations cover the main themes of each chakra. Feel free to invoke some themes but not others. You're also welcome to add any themes that are appropriate for a particular chakra. After invoking, hold passive awareness in the appropriate chakra.

First Chakra (Root, Muladhara)

For healing: *"Spirit that I am, please clear all energetic blocks to my **security, safety,** and **physical well-being**, to the greatest extent that serves highest good, this or something better, thank you."*

To call in energy: *"Maximum **security, safety,** and **physical well-being** that serve highest good, please."*

Second Chakra (Sacral, Svadhishthana)

For healing: *"Spirit that I am, please clear all energetic blocks to my **healthy sexuality** and **abundant creativity**, to the greatest extent that serves highest good, this or something better, thank you."*

To call in energy: *"Maximum **healthy sexuality** and **abundant creativity** that serve highest good, please."*

Third Chakra (Solar Plexus, Manipura)

For healing: *"Spirit that I am, please clear all energetic blocks to my **personal power** and **self-esteem**, to the greatest extent that serves highest good, this or something better, thank you."*

To call in energy: *"Maximum **personal power** and **self-esteem** that serve highest good, please."*

Personal power comes in two basic flavors: "power over" and "shared power."

A "power over" person uses domination and control to get what they want. They're not concerned about any harm their actions might cause unless that harm interferes with their selfish interests.

A "shared power" person gains power so they can do good in the world. They want everything they do to be win-win, with everybody benefiting from their actions.

May you use these Third Chakra invocations and all the information in this book in a "shared power" way!

Fourth Chakra (Heart, Anahata)

For healing: *"Spirit that I am, please clear all energetic blocks to my **compassion, unconditional love,** and **forgiveness**, to the greatest extent that serves highest good, this or something better, thank you."*

To call in energy: *"Maximum **compassion, unconditional love** and **forgiveness** that serve highest good, please."*

Fifth Chakra (Throat, Vishuddha)

For healing: *"Spirit that I am, please clear all energetic blocks to my **clear communication** and **authentic self-expression**, to the greatest extent that serves highest good, this or something better, thank you."*

To call in energy: *"Maximum **clear communication** and **authentic self-expression** that serve highest good, please."*

Sixth Chakra (Third Eye, Ajna)

For healing: *"Spirit that I am, please clear all energetic blocks to my **intuition** and **inner awareness**, to the greatest extent that serves highest good, this or something better, thank you."*

To call in energy: *"Maximum **intuition** and **inner awareness** that serve highest good, please."*

Why say "inner awareness" instead of "inner vision" or "psychic sight"? Because sight is only one of the many ways you might perceive the inner worlds with your sixth chakra.

In my experience, seeing and feeling are the same sense in the inner worlds. Some people lean more toward feeling, while others have a primarily visual experience.

Don't feel bad if, like me, you're better at inner feeling than seeing. The first spiritual teacher I followed actually *preferred* feeling. He liked to say, "If you see it, you're still outside it. But if you feel it, you're one with it!"

Enhanced versions of sound, smell, and taste also exist in the inner worlds. There are also other modes of perception that only exist in the higher dimensions, and are difficult or impossible to describe in words. But "inner awareness" covers them all!

Seventh Chakra (Crown, Sahasrara)

For healing: *"Spirit that I am, please clear all energetic blocks to my **spiritual receptivity** and **divine union**, to the greatest extent that serves highest good, this or something better, thank you."*

To call in energy: *"Maximum **spiritual receptivity** and **divine union** that serve highest good, please."*

No Limit, No Waiting

We've covered a lot of IDA Invocations in this book! Fortunately, **there's no limit to how many you can do in one session**. And **there's no need to wait a certain amount of time between them**. As soon as one invocation is complete, you can do another as soon as you wish. Stop when you run out of time, or when you feel complete with that session.

Four More Healing Stories

There were healing stories in Chapters Three and Five. Here are four more to inspire you!

Emily Heals Major Childhood Trauma with the Healing Invocation

The Healing Invocation helped me profoundly during a time when I was coping with a betrayal. This betrayal just happened to correspond with major childhood traumas.

The betrayal was a doozy! Life was incredibly difficult after it happened. Grief, sadness, and anger would come up constantly while I was just trying to live daily life. I was experiencing extreme levels of mental, emotional, and physical pain. Reality felt distorted.

I couldn't understand what was happening, or look at it clearly. I've always been really calm and collected in stressful situations. But now, that wasn't the case. For the first time, I didn't feel in control of myself. I couldn't rest or concentrate. There was a constant barrage of racing negative thoughts, like a tape playing through my head all the time.

My body was reacting to shock. I felt trapped. My chest and heart hurt every day. I couldn't take a full breath.

This affected my ability to eat and exacerbated a neurological condition that I already suffer from. I developed a tremor from the prolonged stress. Unpredictable surges of sadness and disbelief were the most crippling.

All this would shut me down when I tried to do even the smallest task, even just trying to do dishes or work. I don't normally cry a lot, but I was overwhelmed by crying episodes.

This loss of control felt like it would never end. I've never had so many deep-rooted traumas flare up at once! It was extremely difficult.

I felt like a prisoner to the chatter in my head. I was constantly questioning, angry, and sad. I was terrified because it was affecting my health so greatly. I couldn't find a balance, and I didn't want to be totally taken out by the situation. It was just a mess.

And that's where the Healing Invocation comes in.

The Healing Invocation was such a blessing. I was able to use it during the surges of pain. It would change the energy of the situation and leave me in a much better mental and physical state.

After speaking the words, I would hold my attention in the areas of the greatest pain. My chest area had the most issues. The pain, the tightness, the tears, all that raw emotion — thankfully, everything would start to calm down.

Over time, I felt less and less triggered by the details of the situation. I could handle more of it without it just collapsing me. Before that the pain had felt unbearable.

I used the words: *"Maximum healing that serves highest good, please."* Almost immediately after speaking those words I felt all that pain and negative energy start to move and flush out. Sometimes it only took a few minutes until I felt better. Other times, I would spend maybe twenty minutes, really staying with the situation and working with it until I felt peace.

Even when I wasn't having an acute emotional flare-up, I knew I needed to keep flushing this pain. So, I would use the invocation proactively to keep things from building up. Over time, the Healing Invocation has brought down the intensity of all these feelings. Now I can process these challenging feelings much faster than before.

Of course, there are still things I'm working on. But I'm nowhere near as triggered as I was before the invocations. I've regained a lot of stability and peace.

Using Benjamin's invocations regularly has made me feel like I always have a coping tool. This gives me a strong sense of comfort when I'm dealing with such raw trauma. I honestly feel like it has saved extra wear and tear on my mind, body, and spirit.

— Emily

Rose: From "I'm Going to Die if Something Doesn't Change" to "A Monumental List of Life-Altering Changes."

For the entirety of 2019, my first and only prayer to the gods was, "I'm going to die if something doesn't change. I see no way out. If there's a door to a new path, please help me find it."

I'd been working up to five part-time jobs at once, while sometimes also enrolled in college full-time. My parents didn't believe in higher education, but I really needed a college degree to get a more stable, better-paying career.

I've been in the most abusive phase of my life for the last eight years, getting by on two to four hours of sleep per night. So when I was praying to the gods, it was more of a plea bargain.

If I was supposed to keep going for my young daughter, the gods were going to have to do something drastic to make the cycle stop. Because I knew in my bones that my body couldn't go on much longer this way. It was already shutting down.

As fate would have it, I came across Benjamin's *This Week in Astrology* podcast. To say I'd become a skeptic of all things metaphysical, spiritual, or religious is an egregious understatement. But Benjamin was extremely educational, thorough, empathetic, and engaging in every podcast I listened to.

So, I decided to buy myself a reading with the AstroShaman. I was expecting to take it all in like a course on my chart and my life. If I was lucky, maybe I'd discover an arrow to follow on my life compass.

The kicker is, I don't really remember much about the astrology! When Benjamin asked if I wanted to do his Healing Invocation, I was hesitant. I wondered how much time it would take away from the educational portion of the reading. But I knew I needed a healing and talked my inner critic into saying yes.

What I remember most about that session with Benjamin was the feeling of a door opening for me. **After I did his invocation, it felt like God rushing in!**

This was a major breakthrough because my relationship with God has been difficult. The evangelist political doomsday cult my mother brought me up in brainwashed me into believing that I am forever an unworthy sinner. It taught me that when things were going poorly in my life, it was because I wasn't being a good enough servant of God.

When I was a child I would go to the front of the church at every altar call to be saved. I would beg God to forgive me, to make me better, to have mercy on me. To help me know that I would be forgiven and that I was saved, even as worthless and irredeemable as I was.

I never felt saved. But I did have profound spiritual experiences: visions and voices and life-saving moments where God stepped in throughout my life. So, I knew what God-source energy feels like. I had just never felt it *when I asked* before.

I thought maybe this was because I had done really unthinkable, horrible things in past lives. But **my invocation session opened the door to divine bliss. And it was so effortless!**

Since experiencing Benjamin's invocations, I have undergone a monumental list of life-altering changes — including cutting off all communications with my mother for the very first time in my life! I may be broke and broken, but I am miraculously connected to that healing God-source.

I'm not going to blow sunshine up anybody's skirt and say that Benjamin's invocations have *completely* changed my life. I can't say that I know exactly what I'm doing, or take perfect care of myself, or have wonderful relationships with everyone I love.

But when I do the invocation, I know that I am enough. And it gives me just that little bit of light on my compass to see the arrow toward the door. And I resolve to take the next baby step in my daily practice... which has truly revolutionized the trajectory of my life path!

— Rose Vanyo

Brian: Healing Childhood Wounds 80 Percent More Effectively

This last year was the most challenging and tumultuous time of my life, both emotionally and physically. Working with Benjamin's incredibly helpful invocations has taken me to a whole new level in my journey!

His Embodied Awakening Invocation has greatly helped my intuitive ability. I've been innately intuitive my whole life, but I'm finally able to trust in my intuition 100 percent.

This invocation allows me to connect to my higher power and intuition more effortlessly. It lets me experience more ease, flow, grace, and harmony with the universe.

Benjamin's Healing Invocation has also helped me tremendously. The very first time I used it, it helped me deal with some childhood wounding I'd put on the back burner. The invocation brought the wounding to the surface, then completely dissipated its traumatic energy. *When I try to feel my previous emotional connection to it, it no longer exists!*

I was able to heal this childhood wounding very smoothly, effectively, and quickly. In fact, **the Healing Invocation has helped me about 80 percent more effectively than any other healing tool or technique I've tried!**

So, I'm a huge advocate for Benjamin's invocations. I thank him immensely for not only helping me but so many others through his invocations. I pray and hope that they can bless as many people as possible throughout the world.

— Brian Scotti

Amanda Can Drum Again... and Breathe Without Pain

> Benjamin's invocations helped me with two physical challenges. I love playing my drum, but physical pain had stopped me from playing it for five long years. But a few months after starting the invocations, I had the urge to pick it up again.
>
> I drummed for over half an hour. This was a miracle because I hadn't been able to play for so long. And, amazingly, there was *no pain* while I was drumming!
>
> My other physical challenge was breathing. I smoked for many years and my lungs were so damaged I couldn't take a deep breath. It hurt just to breathe!
>
> But after doing the invocations for a few months, I was walking on the beach one morning and suddenly realized that I was taking deep, full breaths — with no pain.
>
> — Amanda Elwell

No "Extras" Needed

In most of these stories, folks use the IDA Invocations simply and straightforwardly. They don't use additional healing tools like crystals, incense, or music.

"Extras" like these definitely have their place. I use them in my shamanic and spiritual work, and there's nothing wrong with adding them to your invocation work.

But *you don't have to*. The IDA Invocations work just fine on their own. The words, followed by your passive awareness, are all you need.

In Chapter Eight, "Consistency and Amnesia," you learned some ways to stay consistent with your invocation practice. Next, we'll dive deeper into more great ways to stay on track!

CHAPTER ELEVEN: SUPPORT TO STAY ON TRACK

In Chapter Eight you learned how hard it can be to stick with a new habit. In this chapter you'll learn several ways to stay on track with the IDA invocations. And most of them are free!

Free IDA Invocations PDF/Wallet Card

Would you like a handy way to have the most important IDA invocations close at hand? They're on a free PDF at InstantDivineAssistance.com, which you can download to your phone or other device.

There's also a PDF you can print to make a physical wallet card. You can do "budget lamination" by sticking clear tape (I prefer packing tape) to both sides.

Record Your Progress

Make a note every time you do your daily invocation practice. You could do this with a paper or electronic calendar, journal, chalk marks on a wall, or any other system you choose. This could be anything from a simple checkmark to a detailed description of what you experienced that day.

This will make you feel good every time you do it. And a part of you will want to keep your streak going! This is a simple and psychologically proven way to help keep yourself on track.

Reminder Emails

You learned about my free reminder emails in Chapter Eight. Here's the most important information from that section:

These automated reminders give you email support, for as long as you choose, to help you make embodied awakened your daily reality. And they're free!

The emails will be brief. You can easily stop or start these messages, or switch between the four options, whenever you wish. And most feature two-line poems with a variety of inspiring messages.

You have four options to choose from:

> Four Daily Reminders, sent at 8 a.m., 12 p.m., 4 p.m., and 8 p.m.
>
> Four Daily Reminders, sent at 6 a.m., 10 a.m., 2 p.m., and 6 p.m.

Two Daily Reminders, sent at 8 a.m. and 4 p.m.

Two Daily Reminders, sent at 6 a.m. and 2 p.m.

Sign up for these free email reminders at InstantDivineAssistance.com.

IDA Invocation Challenges

I've also created the **IDA Invocation Challenges** to support you.

These start with simple goals you can accomplish easily. When you're ready, you can graduate to more ambitious challenges. These provide even greater rewards!

Level 1 Challenges: Embodied Awakening

Maintain embodied awakening as consistently as you can. Start the day with the Embodied Awakening Invocation, then repeat it as needed throughout the day.

Level 2 Challenges: Embodied Awakening and Healing

This includes Level 1, plus:

Do at least one Healing Invocation each day. This can be in response to a challenge that shows up on its own. Alternatively, you can proactively bring up a past trauma or invoke a "next in line" healing.

Level 3 Challenges: Embodied Awakening, Healing and Custom Invocations

This includes Levels 1 and 2, plus:

Do at least one custom invocation each day. Call in the

energy or consciousness you most desire!

Level 4 Challenges: Embodied Awakening, Healing, Custom, and Hollow Reed Invocations

This includes Levels 1, 2, and 3, plus:

Do at least one Hollow Reed Invocation each day. Flow highest good energy to one or more people or situations. Optional: if you feel ready, flow highest good energy to an "adversarial ally."

You'll get a free email reminder at 6 a.m. each day for the challenge you choose. At the end of each challenge, you can repeat it or advance to the longer challenge at that level. Each level has versions for three or seven days.

When you complete a level's seven-day challenge, you can repeat it or advance to the next level if you're ready. You can also choose any challenge at any time.

Try one of these free challenges now at InstantDivineAssistance.com!

Get an Accountability Partner

As I said in Chapter Eight, once you experience the benefits of the Instant Divine Assistance Invocations, you may feel inspired to share them with others. It's easiest to stay on track if a friend or loved one is doing them with you as your accountability partner.

It's ideal if they're willing to read this book, but that's not absolutely necessary. You can also point them to **"Instant Divine Assistance: Your Free Guide to Fast and Easy Awakening and Healing"** at **astroshaman.com/invocations.** There, they'll learn the basics of the IDA Invocations.

Download the Free Bonus Chapter: "Overcoming Invocation Roadblocks"

Over the years, I've seen many people get excited about the IDA Invocations, but then stop doing them. Many common roadblocks can lead to this unfortunate dead end.

I encourage you to download the free bonus chapter that describes these roadblocks… and tells you how to overcome each one! These roadblocks include:

> Fear of overwhelm.
>
> Worry about losing a relationship, job, or life situation.
>
> Fear of losing control.
>
> A part of you that resists the invocations is dominating other parts that want to do them.
>
> You didn't stick with a previous spiritual path and are afraid you won't stick with this one either.
>
> You don't believe there's *any* spiritual path that will work for you.
>
> You think you're not smart or skillful enough to do the invocations.
>
> Some bad experience made you believe you're cursed or not worthy of awakening.
>
> You think awakening is too hard or takes too long.

You're afraid these invocations are some kind of scam, or fear that I'm trying to take advantage of you.

You don't want to step onto an awakening path without a precise vision of where it will lead.

You think these invocations won't work for you because you don't believe in God.

You can't imagine who you'd be without your trauma and are afraid to find out.

Energetic sensitivity is a challenge for you, and you're afraid the IDA Invocations would make it even worse.

If you recognize any of these obstacles in yourself, don't feel bad. They're more common than you might imagine and are nothing to be embarrassed about.

I've helped many people overcome these obstacles. Learn how you can also master them in my bonus chapter! Get it now for free at InstantDivineAssistance.com.

Subscribe to My Podcast

My *Awaken Heal and Thrive!* podcast launched the same week as this book, and will dive deep into the IDA Invocations. I'll share stories and revelations from my ayahuasca and other plant spirit journeys. And my guests and I will enlighten you with lots of other helpful spiritual insights and experiences.

Subscribe to *Awaken Heal and Thrive!* in your podcast app!

Do My Free Zoom Events

As I mentioned in Chapter Six, you're welcome to join my online group events. I'm repeating that section here for your convenience.

As of this writing, I do a free public Zoom call on the first Monday of each month at 8:00 p.m. US Eastern Time. It's called "New Earth Support Team."

We first create a sacred container and invoke embodied awakening. Then we let our divine allies of love and light know we've come to serve the great global awakening. They take it from there! Our spiritual service is routinely rewarded with personal healing, spiritual upgrades, and profound bliss.

I also offer another free group call, which offers you a direct experience of healing and/or awakening, during the second half of each month. You're always welcome to join us.

To see the current schedule and Zoom info, go to AstroShaman.com. Scroll down the home page to my blog section. There, you'll always find a post for the current month's Awakening Plus events.

These calls are associated with my "Awakening Plus" online membership for spiritual support. Speaking of which....

Join "Awakening Plus"

"Awakening Plus," my online membership, will support your embodied awakening, healing, and divine service. Our motto is, "Awaken, Heal, and Thrive!" (Sound familiar? I like this motto so much that I also used it for the name of my podcast!)

Many members have maintained their "Awakening Plus" memberships for years because their daily reality looks more and more like this:

You flow through life with harmony, ease, and grace. Your human self is comfortably merged with your higher self — all day, every day. This exquisite state is your "new normal."

Suffering? It's a distant memory. Mental chatter and challenging emotions hardly ever happen, and you clear them easily when they do. "Flow state" is your customary consciousness. Intuitive guidance comes as easily as your next breath.

You know why you're here on earth. You live your life with clear purpose and abundant joy. You have awakened... and your awakening keeps blossoming into even more awesome, ecstatic states.

*Before your awakening, you might have said, "It doesn't get any better than this." Now you say, "It **always** gets better!"*

I and your fellow Awakening Plus members can help you with a two-part solution:

1. IDA Invocations

You already know about the Instant Divine Assistance Invocations. They're what this book is about! They're part of most "Awakening Plus" events, and underpin many of our courses.

2. So Much Support!

You'll also get help from the "Awakening Plus" support network. This will help you sustain and deepen your embodied awakening. You can use this support to keep your awakened state thriving and deepening.

Awakening Plus events range from bubble bath gentle to

shamanically intense! They support your individual healing and awakening, as well as global spiritual awakening. We also have community-focused events where members ask questions and connect with each other.

Hundreds of satisfied members make up our supportive online community. Would Awakening Plus also be a good fit for you? Members receive these exclusive benefits:

At least 9 of our monthly Zoom events are members-only. Some members attend lots of live events, while some don't do any.

Many members prefer to experience our events when it's best for them, choosing from an archive of over 500 life-transforming experiences. Amazingly, the recorded events are just as powerful as the live ones!

We even have a "Best of" Guide. This helps you quickly and easily choose the events that are best for you.

Awakening Plus also offers you:

"Instant Divine Assistance: Fast and Easy Awakening and Healing" course

"Self-Guided Internal Family Systems Therapy" course

"Your Divine Allies: Let Them Help You More!" course

"Members Helping Members" service

You can pair up with an accountability partner if you wish

Constant support from the Awakening Plus group energy field

And much more.

Learn more at AwakeningPlus.com!

Chapter Twelve awaits you with some final thoughts.

CHAPTER TWELVE: FINAL THOUGHTS

The Instant Divine Assistance Invocations are the most effective method I know for quickly and efficiently calling in embodied awakening, self-healing, and highest good energy for others… as well as any other energy you want.

I've found nothing that does this more quickly, easily, and effectively. If you know something that works better, please let me know at benjamin@astroshaman.com.

Are these invocations the best techniques you currently have for what they do? If so, I suggest you keep using them as long as that's true. If you find something that works better, use it instead.

But even if you love the IDA Invocations, I suggest you keep doing any other spiritual practices that remain helpful. I also encourage you to periodically evaluate them. No matter how much they've helped you in the past, be willing to release any whose benefits don't justify the time and energy they require now.

The Paths I've Left Behind

Let me illustrate this point with a personal story. When I was in my early forties, I spent about five years practicing Vipassana Buddhism. My main practice was "just sitting." The idea was to simply be with whatever came up, with no resistance. Any thought that emerged was okay. So was any feeling or physical sensation.

At the time, this was a major breakthrough for me. I had spent the previous 20 years attending a meditation school with a highly technical focus. One technique involved about 150 steps, built multiple overlapping structures in the inner dimensions, and took two hours to complete! We were also taught to keep all our chakras tightly sealed to avoid infiltration by dark entities.

So, I was mostly in my head and out of touch with my emotions. Vipassana opened the door for me to finally start feeling the suppressed pain from my childhood. My Great Onion of Consciousness started to peel, and I was able to start feeling more happiness.

I was all-in on Vipassana! I even attended a couple of 10-day silent retreats. I couldn't imagine a more satisfying spiritual path….

Until 2006, when I sat in my first plant spirit ceremony. Drinking the psychoactive juice of the San Pedro cactus blew my doors of perception off their hinges. That single dusk-to-dawn ceremony gave me a more vivid experience of the inner worlds than the entire 20 years I'd spent at that meditation school.

I was also stunned at the amount of healing I experienced that night, and how fast it happened. It felt like I'd been yanked from Vipassana's meandering stroll to a starship hurtling through hyperspace!

After a few San Pedro ceremonies, I discovered another plant spirit medicine called ayahuasca. This quickly became my primary plant spirit ally.

For five years, the Mother Vine blasted and blessed me with her tough love. She relentlessly purged my heavy energy and progressively opened my inner awareness. Finally, when I was ready, she gave me the off-the-charts bliss of abiding awakening in 2012. And she's helped me systematically deepen that awakening ever since.

Two Lessons

I'd like to share two lessons from this brief spiritual autobiography.

First, if I'd never ventured beyond my original meditation school or Vipassana, my consciousness wouldn't have evolved as it has. And you wouldn't be reading this book right now. *My previous paths no longer justified the time and energy they required.*

I remain grateful to them both. They served me well at the time, gave me many benefits, and helped me grow in important ways. But I had to put them in the rearview mirror when it was time for me to evolve in ways they couldn't support.

The second point has to do with speed. There are many paths that, like Vipassana, teach you to "just sit" with challenging thoughts and emotions. Given enough time, persistence, and discipline, this approach can bring healing. However, you might have to suffer through some challenging issues for years on end.

San Pedro and ayahuasca have shown me that healing doesn't have to be slow. One night of plant spirit ceremony has often brought me more healing than all five years of my Vipassana practice!

Of course, not everyone is willing or able to do plant spirit ceremonies. Perhaps that's why ayahuasca gave me the Instant Divine Assistance Invocations to share. It's as if she was thinking, "How much of my benefit can I give to someone who *isn't* sitting in one of my ceremonies?"

The IDA Invocations can't compare with the mind-boggling potency of an ayahuasca ceremony. But they function in a similar way to deliver accelerated awakening, healing, and more. And they don't require restrictive diets or trips to Peru!

The slow paths to healing and awakening are the best choice for some people. But for me, at this stage of my journey, I need speed!

What's the rush? We're in the midst of a historic planetary spiritual awakening. As part of this, thousands of years' worth of toxic energies are being flushed up for collective clearing. That's a big part of why everything seems so crazy right now. But this intensity is the necessary prerequisite to humanity's ultimate breakthrough to a more loving and harmonious world.

All lightworkers are being asked to show up and serve to the best of their ability. The game is on and the stakes are high.

That's why time is of the essence. I'm here to help people heal and awaken. The more healed and awakened I am, the better I can serve them. The faster I heal and awaken, the more service I can give, and the more effective that service will be.

If you resonate with this line of thinking, I encourage you to always pursue your own fastest path to healing and awakening. The more you awaken, the more you'll automatically radiate love and light that will help uplift the planet. If you want to go a step further and serve others with your actions, your intuition stands ready to guide you every step of the way!

Thinner Veils Mean Easier Awakening

Many practices were created long ago when the veils between the physical and spiritual realms were much thicker. But now the veils are a lot thinner... and getting thinner every day!

That's why so many people can invoke embodied awakening and have it work the first time — even if they've never meditated before. Years ago, it might have taken years of disciplined effort to reach a similar awakening.

So, you might not have to make the monumental efforts described in some older practices. And who knows? Someday you might establish an awakening so deep and abiding you won't need any techniques at all. (I'm not there yet, but I'm hoping!)

Thank you for taking this journey of healing and awakening with me. I sincerely hope what you've learned here dramatically improves your life. *May your future "new normal" ecstatically surpass the most amazing reality you can imagine today!*

Would you please take a moment, right now, to post your honest review of this book on Amazon? It would mean the world to me! Your review will make it easier for people to discover this book and be helped by it. Thank you!

Just go to **astroshaman.com/bookreview**. You'll be redirected to the page on Amazon where you can review this book!

APPENDIX A: THE MAIN INVOCATIONS IN THIS BOOK

Embodied Awakening Invocation: "Maximum embodied awakening that serves highest good, please."

Healing Invocation: "Maximum healing that serves highest good, please."

Four ways to use it:

1. When you get triggered.

2. Proactively recall an unhealed trauma.

3. Next in line.

4. Two-Story Thought House.

Hollow Reed Invocation: "Spirit that I am, please flow the energy through me to serve [name of the person(s) or situation(s)]'s highest good."

Custom Invocations: "Maximum [fill in the blank] that serves highest good, please."

The Embodied Awakening Invocation Cycle:

1. "Spirit that I am, please saturate me with the maximum light and divine consciousness that serve highest good, this or something better, thank you."

2. "Spirit that I am, please merge me with the peacefulness of my higher self at its level, to the greatest extent that serves highest good, this or something better, thank you."

3. "Spirit that I am, please integrate my physical and spiritual bodies to the greatest extent that serves highest good, thank you."

4. "Spirit that I am, please grant me the most strong, consistent, and ever-deepening embodied awakening that serves highest good, this or something better, thank you."

Download your free IDA Invocations PDF/wallet card at InstantDivineAssistance.com.

APPENDIX B: KEY TAKEAWAYS

After your first reading, these Key Takeaways can help you review the most important information in Chapters Two through Eleven.

They can also be helpful when you reread this book. You might get what you need just from the Key Takeaways. This would keep you from having to reread an entire chapter.

◆ ◆ ◆

Key Takeaways from "Chapter Two: The Embodied Awakening Invocation"

The Embodied Awakening Invocation has four major benefits:

1. You'll enjoy more harmony, flow, ease, and grace. Instead of being overwhelmed by thoughts and challenging emotions, you'll stay more consistently calm.

2. Whatever you're responsible for, you'll do *more*

responsibly — and more joyfully!

3. Instead of having to always figure things out in your mind, you'll increasingly know what to do through intuition.

4. You'll experience more euphoria!

In embodied awakening, your higher self "drives"... but only with your ego's consent.

Your ego is in no danger and can regain control anytime it wants.

The idea is to housebreak your ego, not destroy it.

The free recording of me leading you into embodied awakening, at InstantDivineAssistance.com, will probably make this invocation easier at first.

Your body position when you do the Embodied Awakening Invocation doesn't matter, as long as you can focus your attention.

If you aren't comfortable calling on your higher self, you can invoke an external divine being such as Jesus Christ or your guardian angel.

The Embodied Awakening Invocation is: **"Maximum embodied awakening that serves highest good, please."**

If you can feel subtle energy moving in your body, hold passive awareness of it during the invocation process. Otherwise, hold passive awareness of your breath coming and going on its own.

While the invocation is filling you with energy...

> Don't make anything happen with effort or willpower.

Don't *stop* anything from happening.

Don't *deliberately* visualize or imagine anything.

If a distraction arises,

> Don't fight it.
>
> Don't try to change it.
>
> Let it be exactly as it is, with no resistance.

After noting a distraction, relax back into your chosen focus: subtle energy or breath.

Play the Minimum Effort Game: use the least possible effort (which might be no effort at all) that keeps your focus on subtle energy or breath.

When you're in embodied awakening, four things will be true at the same time:

1. No mental chatter.
2. No challenging emotion.
3. You'll feel peaceful.
4. All this will be completely effortless.

You may also notice tingling in your body.

There's a subtle change in your perception.

Partial awakening is better than none!

Key Takeaways from Chapter Three: The Healing Invocation

The "Great Onion of Consciousness" explains how doing effective shadow work speeds up your spiritual awakening.

Part of your higher self animates your human body, while the rest of it watches from above and drops hints (intuition).

If you're like most humans, you're "behind the veil" and chose some degree of spiritual amnesia.

Your higher self chose certain past-life wounds and traumas for this lifetime, as well as specific gifts and talents.

Your human self would describe the everyday reality of your higher self with words like ecstasy, bliss, and euphoria.

Every unhealed wound or trauma, from this life or a past life, puts a dark layer around the luminous core of your higher self.

These layers built up so that your soul looks like an onion.

The ecstatic core of your higher self is at the center, surrounded by dark layers of unhealed pain.

Some of that divine light shines through the onion, but the dark layers of pain block the rest.

The Healing Invocation peels these layers one by one.

Every time a layer peels off, the light seems brighter to your human self.

Even peeling one layer can open you to a profound new level of euphoria!

Your ego calls in healing from your higher self, which does it while your human self passively receives it.

Notice anything that doesn't feel wonderful. It could be physical, emotional, or both.

If you can't find anything, deliberately recall a past trauma that brings up challenging feelings.

You'll never feel overwhelmed while doing this or any other IDA Invocation.

Put your attention on the challenging feeling.

Give it a zero-to-10 rating on the intensity scale.

Ignore any thoughts or images that arise.

If you get distracted, refocus on the challenging feeling.

Say the Healing Invocation out loud if you can, silently if you must: **"Maximum healing that serves highest good, please."**

Let the words go and rest your attention on the challenging sensation.

Focus on the central point of intensity if it has one. Focus more broadly if it doesn't.

Use the minimum effort that gives you complete awareness of the challenging feeling.

If heavy energy wants to exit your body, let it leave.

If heavy energy wants to transmute to love and light, let it.

If challenging energy moves around, track it like a hound dog until it completely leaves your energy field.

If energy that's more challenging arises elsewhere, you can shift your attention there instead.

If you can easily hold attention on more than one challenged area at a time, that's okay if it speeds up your healing process.

The challenging energy will gradually decrease, while euphoric energy increases.

Eventually, the euphoria will outweigh the challenge.

If you let a healing round run its full course, you'll usually feel no discomfort and lots of euphoria! Your physical body may feel more like energy than solid matter.

Are you experiencing euphoria, and don't feel any more heavy energy being processed? Then that healing round is complete. Chances are that your discomfort is either gone or significantly reduced.

If your challenge is completely gone, go on about your business.

If some discomfort remains, and you have a little more time, it's best to do another healing round.

Additional rounds usually go much faster than the first one.

Some things can heal, while others can't. Some souls must learn how to gracefully accept and adapt to a situation.

The Healing Invocation is always worth a try to see if it can clear a particular challenge.

Key Takeaways from Chapter Four: IDA Invocation Daily Maintenance

First thing each morning, as soon as you think about it, do the Embodied Awakening Invocation: **"Maximum embodied awakening that serves highest good, please."**

Passively feel subtle energy or breath until your higher self merges with your human self.

Ask yourself the confirmation question. Is there peacefulness with no mental chatter or challenging emotion, all with no effort? If so, go on about your business.

Your embodied awakening could lock in within five or ten seconds.

If your embodied awakening slips, simply do its invocation again — anytime, anywhere, anyplace. **Do it as needed, not on a fixed schedule.**

Refresh it right away so you don't fall into spiritual amnesia!

Use the Healing Invocation when the Embodied Awakening invocation isn't enough to free you from mental chatter or challenging emotion.

Once you're triggered, invoke the Healing Invocation as soon as possible.

Process as much heavy energy as time permits. You can always do another healing round later if needed.

The specific layer of heavy energy you flush or transmute is gone forever!

Here's the briefest possible summary of daily maintenance with the IDA Invocations:

First thing each morning, do the Embodied Awakening Invocation: **"Maximum embodied awakening that serves highest good, please."**

Repeat as needed throughout the day.

If you get triggered more strongly, use the Healing Invocation: **"Maximum healing that serves highest good, please."**

Key Takeaways from Chapter Five: Four Ways to Use the Healing Invocation

If something stirs you up, use the basic Healing Invocation: **"Maximum healing that serves highest good, please."**

Passively witness the challenging phenomenon while your higher self takes care of it for you.

Or you can deliberately bring up an old trauma from your past. Once you feel its challenging energy, ask your higher self to heal it for you.

A third way to use the Healing Invocation is to heal whatever's next in line.

You can completely heal a trauma without knowing anything about it.

To do this, say to your higher self, **"Maximum healing that serves highest good, please."**

Let your higher self bring up whatever heavy energy is next in line.

Once you notice a challenging sensation, passively rest your attention there.

Let the Healing Invocation proceed as usual.

There's no risk of missing important life lessons, even if you don't know anything about the heavy energy you're processing.

There are many effective, feeling-based healing methods that don't require cognitive understanding.

I've seen no evidence that awareness of what's being released makes a healing more beneficial.

There are aspects of healing and awakening that a human intellect can never understand.

There isn't always a lesson associated with every healing experience.

During or after a healing, your higher self will give you any thoughts or images about it that serve your highest good.

The Thought-Focused Healing Invocation specifically targets persistent mental chatter.

A thought is like a virus. It's a partial life form. Without a host to draw energy from, it can't replicate itself and create more thought-forms.

You are pure consciousness, but you have a community of thought-forms that help you think.

In the Two-Story Thought House visualization, you start with your thoughts on the ground floor.

Walk up the stairs to the second-floor balcony. From there, you can see the thoughts on the first floor.

Give the chattering thoughts your full attention. Then say, **"Maximum healing that serves highest good, please."**

You are pure awareness. Simply witness what the thoughts are doing on their own.

As you do this, the thoughts slow down, stop, and dissolve. This leaves you with a clear, spacious mind.

Here are four ways you can use the Healing Invocation:

> 1. You get triggered by something and experience a challenging physical or emotional sensation. Say, **"Maximum healing that serves highest good, please."** Then gently focus on the challenging feeling while your higher self heals it for you.
>
> 2. Deliberately recall an unhealed trauma to get it stirred up. Then say the Healing Invocation and focus as described above. You can systematically heal your old traumas by doing this.
>
> 3. Say the Healing Invocation, then let your higher self bring up the next trauma in line to be healed. Wait until you feel a challenge arise, then focus on it and follow the usual procedure.
>
> 4. To eliminate unrelenting thoughts, use the Healing Invocation with the Two-Story Thought House visualization

Key Takeaways from Chapter Six: The Hollow Reed Invocation: How to Be a Conduit for Highest Good Energy

With the Hollow Reed Invocation, you can effortlessly act as a conduit to flow highest good energy to others.

Note how your body and subtle energy feel.

Decide where you want highest good energy to flow. It can be to one or more people or situations.

When first learning this, I suggest you start with someone you love or like.

Say, **"Spirit that I am, please flow the energy through me to serve [name of the person(s) or situation(s)]'s highest good."**

After you say the words, let them go and passively feel energy or breath.

Don't deliberately visualize anything.

Don't use any effort to flow energy.

You don't have to use your hands.

Just be a passive pipeline: "I conduit!"

You may notice subtle energy flowing into your crown chakra and out the front of your body to your recipient(s).

If you feel this energy, let it flow on its own. Otherwise, rest in passive breath awareness.

You don't have to worry about the color of the energy, what

spiritual plane(s) it's coming from, or which spiritual allies are helping. Your higher self has all this covered.

You'll probably feel significantly *better* after the energy flow. What you give, you automatically receive. One of the quickest ways to feel better is to invoke highest good energy for others!

When you flow energy to others using this IDA Invocation, you don't have to know their highest good and don't need their permission. As long as you only call in *highest good* energy, no harm or karmic violation can occur.

Even with the best intentions, you may not know what another person's highest good is.

Sometimes a suffering human needs to develop the strength to solve a major challenge on their own.

When appropriate, you would ideally exercise such wise restraint with deep compassion and unconditional love.

If you force something to happen, you could unintentionally cause harm even if you're only trying to help.

It's safest to only ask for highest good energy to flow.

The Karma-Free Safety Clause is: *"To the greatest extent that serves highest good, this or something better, thank you."*

Once you get comfortable flowing energy to people you like or love, you can flow highest good energy to people who trigger you.

This can stir up unhealed emotional wounds that this person triggers.

If you feel discomfort after the energy flow wraps up, you can do a Healing Invocation for yourself to help clear it.

The catalyst these "adversarial allies" bring to your life can help speed up your personal evolution.

You can have advanced Hollow Reed experiences once you reach a certain level of awakening.

Here are the two ways you can use the Hollow Reed Invocation to flow highest good energy to another person:

1. **Safest:** Simply invoke highest good energy.

2. **Still safe, but be careful:** ask for the specific outcome you want, but close with the Karma-Free Safety Clause.

Key Takeaways from Chapter Seven: Invocation Construction Kit

You can create new invocations whenever you like: just plug the right words into a simple formula.

You can ask for whatever shift of energy or consciousness you desire.

Here's the formula:

1. Start with the word "Maximum."

2. Describe the energy shift you want. Use simple, clear language.

3. Add "to the greatest extent that serves highest good, please."

4. Close with "this or something better, thank you."

Or use this shortcut: **"Maximum [fill in the blank] that serves highest good, please."**

You can play with any or all of these custom invocations:

Spiritual Awakening Invocation

Peace of Mind Invocation

Light Body Awareness Invocation

Bliss Invocation

Light Body Expansion Invocation

Rather than getting to a particular outcome through your usual human effort, can you invoke it — and passively receive it — through the grace of your higher self?

The IDA Invocations merge prayer and meditation. This brings you the benefits of both approaches in a single system.

In my experience, the IDA Invocations shift reality faster and more effectively than any affirmations I've encountered.

The Law of Attraction typically focuses on *physical* manifestation, while the IDA Invocations specialize in *energetic* shifts.

You could use these custom invocations to empower your Law of Attraction work:

For clearing: **"Spirit that I am, please clear or transmute any energies blocking what I'm calling in so that my** desired outcome manifests to the greatest extent, and at the fastest rate, that serves highest good."

For energizing: **"Spirit that I am, please saturate me with those energies that will help my desired outcome manifest to the greatest extent, and at the fastest rate, that serves highest good."**

❖ ❖ ❖

Key Takeaways from Chapter Eight: Consistency and Amnesia

If you aren't consistent with your awakening practice, you could slip back into amnesia — without even realizing it!

This could cause you endless suffering and unhappiness.

I strongly recommend that you *never* take a day off from your invocation practice.

You might be able to invoke embodied awakening in just five or ten seconds.

It might only take you five or ten minutes a day to refresh it.

In return, you get to spend your entire day in a magnificent, awakened state!

Without a daily practice, the darkness subtly slips in around the edges. You get more and more covered over and could unknowingly sink back into amnesia.

Plus, persistent daily practice will amplify your euphoria. You're more likely to jump to new levels of awakening more quickly and consistently.

You'll spend much less time making decisions because of your improved intuition. Your daily invocation practice could easily save you hours and lots of effort every day.

An awakened state is the world's best beauty treatment!

You can set recurring alarms on your phone. These can remind you to do the Embodied Awakening Invocation first thing, and check to see if you're in embodied awakening later in the day.

You can work with an accountability partner to help you stay in embodied awakening.

If you do this, it's ideal if they also read this book. Or point them to **"Instant Divine Assistance: Your Free Guide to Fast and Easy Awakening and Healing"** at **https://www.astroshaman.com/invocations/**.

If you don't begin a new habit immediately, chances are you never will.

My free automated invocation reminders give you email support, for as long as you choose, to help you make embodied awakened your daily reality. Sign up at InstantDivineAssistance.com.

What if, despite your best efforts, you *do* slip into amnesia… and the Embodied Awakening Invocation doesn't rekindle your divine awareness? In this order:

    1. On your own, do the full Embodied Awakening Invocation Cycle described in Chapter Nine.

    2. If that doesn't work, use the

Embodied Awakening Invocation Cycle recording at InstantDivineAssistance.com. My voice will guide you through the process.

3. If even that doesn't do it, get an awakened person to help you. I do this for clients in my Shamanic Healing/ IFS sessions (https://www.astroshaman.com/services/shamanic-healing/).

◆ ◆ ◆

Key Takeaways from Chapter Nine: The Embodied Awakening Invocation Cycle

To enjoy the deepest possible experience, use the free recording I made of this cycle at InstantDivineAssistance.com.

There are four invocations in this cycle:

1. Your higher self saturates you with the maximum light and divine consciousness that serve highest good.

2. You merge with your higher self at its level, experiencing yourself as pure blissful energy.

3. Your higher self merges with you in your physical body.

4. You ask to consistently maintain the consciousness of your higher self from now on, to the greatest extent that serves highest good, with optimal physical functionality.

There's a richness and sweetness to this longer process you don't get with the shortcut.

Most notably — and blissfully! — this cycle gives you a chance to merge with your higher self in its spiritual realm.

You might also deepen your awakening during the fourth invocation.

You might find it especially helpful if you read the rest of this chapter *after* you work with the recording of the Embodied Awakening Invocation Cycle at InstantDivineAssistance.com.

The rest of this chapter is especially helpful if you want to do the cycle on your own, without the recording.

Here's the first invocation: **"Spirit that I am, please saturate me with the maximum light and divine consciousness that serves highest good, this or something better, thank you."** This is the *Maximum Light and Divine Consciousness Invocation*.

Once you start feeling peaceful, do the second invocation. This is the *"Merge Me With the Peacefulness of My Higher Self at Its Level" Invocation*: **"Spirit that I am, please merge me with the peacefulness of my higher self at its level, to the greatest extent that serves highest good, this or something better, thank you."**

After saying this invocation, shift your awareness to feel peacefulness.

Play the Minimum Effort Game.

As this invocation takes effect, the peacefulness will grow stronger all by itself. Eventually, you'll feel like a cloud of energy or a ball of light.

You'll experience yourself as pure energy. You'll feel exquisitely peaceful. And you won't experience any mental chatter or challenging emotions.

Rest in your peaceful light body. At this level, there's nowhere to go and nothing to do. But it feels amazing!

Next, invoke this longer version of the Embodied Awakening Invocation: "**Spirit that I am, please integrate my physical and spiritual bodies to the greatest extent that serves highest good, this or something better, thank you.**"

Return to passively feeling energy or breath. Use the minimum effort needed to maintain this awareness.

Once you've achieved embodied awakening, ask yourself: Do I prefer the way I feel right now or the way I usually feel every day?

If you prefer how embodied awakening feels, would you like this to become your new normal? *Remember that you can fulfill all your responsibilities* **more** *responsibly, and more joyfully, in this state.*

If you said yes, say the fourth and final invocation in the cycle: "**Spirit that I am, please grant me the most strong, consistent, and ever-deepening embodied awakening that serves highest good, this or something better, thank you.**"

Does your embodied awakening hold steady on its own with your eyes open?

As you swing an arm, do you feel your tingly energy arm moving in sync with your physical arm? Can you feel tingly energy throughout your body?

This completes the four-step invocation cycle. Now you can enjoy the profound benefits of embodied awakening in everything you do!

Key Takeaways from Chapter Ten: Invocations for Specific Challenges

Here are all the invocations from this chapter:

"Maximum **ease of letting go**, to the greatest extent that serves highest good, this or something better, thank you."

"Spirit that I am, **please saturate me with your healing, loving light. Please clear from me all energy that does not serve my highest good**, this or something better, thank you."

"Maximum **clarity of life direction**, to the greatest extent that serves highest good, this or something better, thank you."

"Spirit, **please bring the maximum amount of healing to this relationship**. May this be so to the greatest extent that serves highest good, this or something better, thank you." (RT)

"Spirit, please grant me **the maximum amount of your divine peace and rest**, right now. May this be so to the greatest extent that serves highest good, thank you." (RT)

"Spirit that I am, please **clear the energy of fatigue and sleepiness from my field**, to the greatest extent that serves highest good, this or something better, thank you. "

"Spirit that I am, **maximum alertness, focus and conscious presence** that serve highest good, please."

"Spirit that I am, **please flow through me the maximum amount of your divine peace and love toward [name of person]**. May this be so to the greatest extent that serves highest good, thank you." (RT)

"Spirit that I am, **please flow calming energy through me to help smooth this environment and help improve relations.... Let me be that beacon of light.**" (Anjuli)

"**Maximum embodied awakening** that serves highest good — **with gratitude** [and jazz hands]!" (Sarah)

Anxiety, Generalized Anxiety Disorder (GAD), and **Panic Disorder (PD):** "Maximum **calmness** that serves highest good, this or something better, thank you."

Social Anxiety Disorder (SAD): "Maximum **calmness and confidence in social situations** that serve highest good, this or something better, thank you."

Specific Phobias: "Maximum **ease and comfort when dealing with [name of phobia]** that serves highest good, this or something better, thank you."

Obsessive-Compulsive Disorder (OCD): "Maximum **ease and flow in doing what I choose** that serves highest good, this or something better, thank you."

Post-Traumatic Stress Disorder (PTSD): "Maximum **healing** that serves highest good, please."

Depression: "Maximum **hopefulness** that serves highest good, please."

Step 7 of a 12-Step program: "Spirit that I am, **remove from me**

every single defect of character which stands in the way of my usefulness to you and my fellows, to the greatest extent that serves highest good, this or something better, thank you."

Step 11 of a 12-Step program: "**Maximum embodied awakening** that serves highest good, please."

1. First Chakra (Root, Muladhara)

For healing: "Spirit that I am, please clear all energetic blocks to my **security, safety,** and **physical well-being**, to the greatest extent that serves highest good, this or something better, thank you."

To call in energy: "Maximum **security, safety,** and **physical well-being** that serve highest good, please."

2. Second Chakra (Sacral, Svadhishthana)

For healing: "Spirit that I am, please clear all energetic blocks to my **healthy sexuality** and **abundant creativity**, to the greatest extent that serves highest good, this or something better, thank you."

To call in energy: "Maximum **healthy sexuality** and **abundant creativity** that serve highest good, please."

3. Third Chakra (Solar Plexus, Manipura)

For healing: "Spirit that I am, please clear all energetic blocks to my **personal power** and **self-esteem**, to the greatest extent that serves highest good, this or something better, thank you."

To call in energy: "Maximum **personal power** and **self-esteem** that serve highest good, please."

4. Fourth Chakra (Heart, Anahata)

For healing: "Spirit that I am, please clear all energetic blocks to my **compassion, unconditional love,** and **forgiveness**, to the greatest extent that serves highest good, this or something better, thank you."

To call in energy: "Maximum **compassion, unconditional love,** and **forgiveness** that serve highest good, please."

5. Fifth Chakra (Throat, Vishuddha)

For healing: "Spirit that I am, please clear all energetic blocks to my **clear communication** and **authentic self-expression**, to the greatest extent that serves highest good, this or something better, thank you."

To call in energy: "Maximum **clear communication** and **authentic self-expression** that serve highest good, please."

6. Sixth Chakra (Third Eye, Ajna)

For healing: "Spirit that I am, please clear all energetic blocks to my **intuition** and **inner awareness**, to the greatest extent that serves highest good, this or something better, thank you."

To call in energy: "Maximum **intuition** and **inner awareness** that serve highest good, please."

7. Seventh Chakra (Crown, Sahasrara)

For healing: "Spirit that I am, please clear all energetic blocks to my **spiritual receptivity** and **divine union**, to the greatest extent that serves highest good, this or something better, thank you."

To call in energy: "Maximum **spiritual receptivity** and **divine union** that serve highest good, please."

This chapter closes with four more healing stories:

1. Emily Heals Major Childhood Trauma with the Healing Invocation

2. Rose: From "'I'm Going to Die if Something Doesn't Change" to "A Monumental List of Life-Altering Changes."

3. Brian: Healing Childhood Wounding 80 Percent More Effectively

4. Amanda Can Drum Again and Breathe Without Pain

Finally, you learned that the IDA Invocations are complete unto themselves and don't need any "extras" to make them effective.

Key Takeaways from Chapter Eleven: Support to Help You Stay on Track

In this chapter, you learned a variety of ways to stay on track with the IDA invocations. And most of them are free!

Reminder Emails.

Four Levels of IDA Invocation Challenges.

Get an Accountability Partner.

Download the Free Bonus Chapter: "Overcoming Invocation Roadblocks."

Subscribe to My New Podcast.

Do My Free Zoom Events.

Join "Awakening Plus."

You can access these resources at InstantDivineAssistance.com.

APPENDIX C: RESOURCES AND WEBSITES MENTIONED IN THIS BOOK

Chapter Three: The Healing Invocation

A Brief History of Time by Stephen Hawking (Bantam Dell Publishing Group, 1988).

Chapter Six: The Hollow Reed Invocation: How to Be a Conduit for Highest Good Energy

Journey of Souls by Michael Newton (Llewellyn, 1994). Revelatory book about how souls plan their next human incarnation.

LawOfOne.info: Free channeled information. Profound explanations of life, the universe, and everything.

Chapter Eight: Consistency and Amnesia

mckinsey.com/business-functions/people-and-organizational-performance/our-insights/decision-making-in-the-age-of-urgency: Post about the inefficiency of much decision-making in business.

Atomic Habits by James Clear (Avery, 2018). Excellent book on creating helpful habits.

entrepreneur.com/article/310062: This post describes how having an accountability partner makes it much more likely that you'll achieve your goals.

"Instant Divine Assistance: Your Free Guide to Fast and Easy Awakening and Healing" at astroshaman.com/invocations/. This is where anyone can learn how to do the Embodied Awakening Invocation and the Healing Invocation, and integrate them into a daily practice. Free!

My Shamanic Healing/IFS sessions: astroshaman.com/services/shamanic-healing/. ("IFS" stands for Internal Family Systems Therapy.)

Chapter Ten: Invocations for Specific Challenges

adaa.org/understanding-anxiety/facts-statistics. This page on the website of the Anxiety & Depression Association of America (ADAA) is the source of my mental health statistics.

mayoclinic.org/diseases-conditions/bipolar-disorder/symptoms-causes/syc-20355955. Mayo Clinic web page that describes the symptoms of bipolar disorder.

Bill W.: "The Big Book." The bible of Alcoholics Anonymous, which I quote in my section on IDA Invocations for 12-Step programs.

Chapter Eleven: Support to Stay on Track

astroshaman.com/awaken-heal-and-thrive: The home page of my *Awaken Heal and Thrive!* podcast.

Multiple Chapters

AwakeningPlus.com: Information about my online membership, "Awakening Plus," that can help you awaken, heal, and thrive!

AstroShaman.com: The site for my individual services, including Astrology+, Shamanic Healing/IFS, and life coaching. AstroShaman.com also features my astrology forecasts, podcasts, videos, blog posts and more.

InstantDivineAssistance.com: Free resources to support your work with the IDA Invocations.

After Chapter Twelve

astroshaman.com/bookreview. This will redirect you to the page on Amazon where you can review this book!

GRATITUDE

It took a village to write this book! Big thanks to all the following:

My wonderful subscribers and followers, who helped me finalize the title and cover design.

My twenty-eight beta readers whose insights *significantly* improved this book, and the BetaBooks.co app that made it easy to work with their feedback.

My enthusiastic launch team, who helped this book get noticed on amazon.

My Reedsy.com editor, Catherine J. Rourke, whose enthusiasm and expertise took this book to the next level.

ProWritingAid.com, the brilliant AI editing app that helped me polish the manuscript before I sent it to Catherine.

Sanjeev Gupta of grafixland.com, who patiently endured my endless revisions to create the striking cover.

My thousands of clients and Awakening Plus members who prove, in their own lives, that the Instant Divine Assistance Invocations work.

My clients and "Awakening Plus" members who so generously contributed their stories to this book.

Chandler Bolt and Joanna Penn, whose excellent books and podcasts on self-publishing were invaluable resources to this first-time author.

Many others whose contributions — direct and indirect, large and small — gave me personal support and helped this book manifest, including my Riverlight Village peeps and ayahuasca co-journeyers. I regret that I can't name you all here, but you know who you are!

My magnificent spiritual allies (whom I describe early in Chapter Three), for making what I do possible.

My life partner and embodied angel Spiritsong, for cheerleading this book, saving my life, helping me grow and evolve, supporting me in endless practical ways, and always showering me with unconditional love. I'm so grateful and fortunate to be with my beloved soulmate again!

ABOUT THE AUTHOR

Benjamin Bernstein is an awakening facilitator, shamanic healer, life coach, and award-winning astrologer. He has done over 10,000 sessions with clients worldwide. He lives near Asheville, NC with his beloved life partner Spiritsong. This is his first book.

His 45-year spiritual path has included Peruvian shamanism, hundreds of ayahuasca ceremonies, and his Instant Divine Assistance (IDA) Invocations. Benjamin devotes special attention to "**Awakening Plus**," his online membership that helps members awaken, heal, and thrive!

Made in the USA
Middletown, DE
25 September 2023

39377390R00113